THE SIX KEYS TO UNLOCK AND EMPOWER YOUR MIND

SPOT LIARS & CHEATS, NEGOTIATE
ANY DEAL TO YOUR ADVANTAGE,
WIN AT THE OFFICE, INFLUENCE
FRIENDS, & MUCH MORE

MARC SALEM

RODALE

© 2007 by Marc Salem

Illustrations © 2007 by Rodale Inc.

All rights reserved. No part of this publication may be reproduced or transmitted
in any form or by any means, electronic or mechanical, including photocopying,
recording, or any other information storage and retrieval system, without the
written permission of the publisher.

Rodale books may be purchased for business or promotional use or for special
sales. For information, please write to:

Special Markets Department, Rodale Inc.,
733 Third Avenue, New York, NY 10017

Printed in the United States of America

Rodale Inc. makes every effort to use acid-free ⊗, recycled paper ♻.

CBS *60 Minutes II* transcript, pages ix to xii, © 2005 CBS Worldwide Inc.
All rights reserved. Originally broadcast on *60 Minutes II* on May 25, 2005,
over the CBS Television Network.

Illustrations by Drew Frantzen

Library of Congress Cataloging-in-Publication Data

Salem, Marc.
    The six keys to unlock and empower your mind : spot liars & cheats,
negotiate any deal to your advantage, win at the office, influence friends
& much more / Marc Salem.
        p.   cm.
    ISBN-13 978–1–59486–559–6 paperback
    ISBN-10 1–59486–559–0 paperback
    1. Mental discipline.   2. Self-help techniques.   I. Title.
BF632.S25   2007
158—dc22   2007004348

Distributed to the book trade by Holtzbrinck Publishers

2   4   6   8   10   9   7   5   3   1   paperpack

In memory
of my loving parents

In loving tribute to my family:
My wife, Tova—You are my muse and rock.
My brothers, Chaim and Avi, and their families—
You are in this book far more than you can know.
The kids and grandkids—You make me
understand hope.

CONTENTS

PREFACE

TRANSCRIPT CBS 60 MINUTES II

MAY 25, 2005

(CBS) **Wallace:** Just about every week, at a theater somewhere in the world, hundreds of skeptical people show up to see for themselves the work and the performance of a man who calls himself a mentalist—a mind reader.

When they leave the theater a couple of hours later, they're astonished. But they can't help but wonder, "How'd he do that?" A while back I was one of those skeptics, too. But after watching, I was hooked.

60 Minutes: We invited a random audience to see Marc Salem perform his magic at the Lyceum Theater in New York and set up cameras onstage for this unusual experiment.

Salem: What I want you to do is select three books, first to work with.

Wallace: . . . one, two, three.

Salem: Excellent, OK . . . Mike, here's what I want you to do. I want you to say stop at any point.

Wallace: Stop.

Salem: OK, look at the first couple of words in that page. . . . Lock those words in your mind. All right. Could you open your book to any page? OK. Hundreds of words facing you right now? Have you got one in mind?

Wallace: I've got one.

Salem: OK, shut the book. I want you to stare at my forehead. It's easy to do, it goes to the back of my neck. See the first letter of the word you're thinking of. Mike, think of the first letter of any of your words. Just focus, Mike, just focus on the letter. Is that an "A"?

Wallace: Yes, it is.

Salem: Excellent.

Salem somehow read Wallace's mind, and he even guessed the woman's first letter, which happened to be "P."

How does he do it? Salem promises that he's not getting any help from hidden cameras or spies in the audience, and he offers $100,000 to anyone who can prove otherwise. His tricks are mind-blowing. Some of them are magic; others make you believe he actually can read your mind.

He was able to guess the serial numbers on a dollar bill from Wallace's wallet. He amazed a doctor from the audience by stopping and starting his pulse at will. He could identify objects while blindfolded. He made the hands on Wallace's watch move from 1:30 p.m. to 2:00 p.m. And he told an audience member whom he had never met where she went on her last vacation.

However he does it, it's hard not to be taken in.

Is he psychic? "No, I don't even know what psychic is. What I do isn't psychic. What I do isn't supernatural," says Salem. "It has absolutely no relation whatsoever to those other realms, whether or not they even exist."

Can he read thoughts? "Yes, I could pick up thoughts," says Salem. "But a thought is not the same thing as a mind, OK? Let me make a distinction. To read a mind means I can go in there and pull out things you don't want me to get. A thought is something that you're focused on."

But if he's not a psychic, how does he explain his strange skills?

"There was a wonderful experiment in the last century. Clever Hans, a horse that everybody thought was able to read thoughts. And people would ask Clever Hans, 'How much is two and two?' And Hans would go four times. And it was amazing and Hans went all around the world," says Salem.

"And then some scientists put blinders on Hans. And suddenly Hans was unable to do it. And it's not that anybody was committing fraud. What it was, everybody would wait with tension till Hans reached the right number, and then relax. And that's when Hans would stop doing that. So I do think that, on that level sometimes, I'm picking up things like a horse."

But it's much more than that. His family always felt that he had some kind of special gift. Salem, whose real name is Moshe Botwinick, was the middle son of a prominent Philadelphia rabbi. As a child, he had a hypersensitivity toward people and his surroundings, always reading into subtle facial expressions and gestures. His family says he would routinely guess what his Hanukkah gift was before opening it, or where his parents were headed on vacation before they could even tell him.

"Even at that age, I think I understood certain things about suggestibility. Certain things about probabilities," says Salem. "And I think I took many a guess about things in the world around me. With limited amounts of information, I make connections that more often than not are correct."

Over time, Salem fine-tuned his skills, including an uncanny ability to tell when someone was lying to him. Whether Salem uses tricks or not, his abilities as a human lie detector have made him valuable off-stage, too. After a former New York City police commissioner saw him perform one night, he was offered a job to train the rank and file how to spot liars.

In 1998 lawyers involved in a big tobacco trial hired him to weed out jurors with hidden biases against smokers. Salem says it's practically impossible to lie to him: "Even the most practiced liar, though, if they have an element of guilt, there's going to be what we call leakage.

"There is going to be information being given off. So, a politician can be trained and trained and trained, and yet their mouth is going to get a little dry when they're lying," adds Salem. "OK. There's gonna be the little bit of an adrenaline rush . . . I would say virtually every thought we have has some physical manifestation."

"So to read somebody's thoughts, you've got to read their bodies?" asks Wallace.

"To read somebody's thoughts, you do need to read their bodies," says Salem.

And that's the key to understanding his mental techniques. Salem believes that if we all used our observational skills better, we could do what he does. We could actually read other people's thoughts.

INTRODUCTION

I've made a career out of tapping the hidden powers of the mind. Considered in the minds of many the world's leading mentalist, I've helped top wheeler-dealers determine whether to accept or reject million-dollar deals during face-to-face business negotiations. I've judged the mind-set of potential jurors in some of the country's biggest and most controversial trials. I've trained some of law enforcement's finest in the art of detecting lies, and have even gone head to head with a polygraph machine and won just by listening intently. And I've stretched the credulity of thousands of audience members with the mental feats I perform in my on- and off-Broadway show called *Mind Games*.

It's not that I'm smarter than all the people who hire me or come to see my show. It's not that I'm smarter than you. I have simply learned to maximize my mental capabilities.

Welcome to the world of mind games. It is my world, but it can be yours as well. By learning how to control your own mind, you can learn to read your own thoughts and those of others as I do. Sound impossible? I've been doing it for years.

I've always been sensitive to other people's thoughts. I used to sit in a dark room with my younger brother and try to guess what number he had in his head. I'm still not quite sure what the process I used was, but I know from experience that ideas, thoughts, and notions can be conveyed from one person to another without being spoken. It could be that I knew my brother so well that I was able to anticipate what the next number he would think of would be. I think it's also true that there's a psychological component—a logic if you will—that dictates such number sequences. (Try it yourself by asking someone to start thinking of numbers. After a minute or two, you're going to be able to anticipate some of those numbers.)

When I was nine, I told my brothers that our parents were planning a surprise family vacation. I had no idea then how I knew that either, but I suspect that I picked up hints within my general environment and processed that information unconsciously. Perhaps I glimpsed a bathing suit or a new toothbrush coming into the house. Perhaps I overheard someone humming a song about the beach. Perhaps something was said between my father and mother out of my earshot that I overheard but didn't consciously process. Whether or not any of those things happened, I'm sure there was a sense of anticipation that I would have picked up on.

As a youngster, I would pull in all this information unintentionally. Once, after a move and before the boxes were all unpacked, my mother wondered aloud where her red hat had been packed. Unhesitatingly, I pointed out the right box. If this had been a once-in-a-lifetime occurrence, my family might have assumed that my "guess" was pure luck. But this sort of thing happened all the time. They, as I, knew that neither luck nor guesswork had anything to do with it. I was simply more attuned to the environment around me than most.

Perhaps because of this facility, how the mind works has always fascinated me. From a young age, I would try to understand why people said things based on a given situation or at a given time, and try to understand through their tone of voice or the way they moved what they were thinking about. I loved to go to train stations and airports to watch people from a distance so I could "listen" to all the information that they were giving off in their gestures, postures, and expressions. My high school friends could usually prod me into giving demonstrations of my intuitive abilities by finding lost items or predicting the teacher's next mental breakdown.

All this honed my perceptions and led me quite naturally to the field of psychology. I studied with Ray Birdwhitsell at the University of Pennsylvania, one of the first researchers to propose the idea that we communicate as much through movement and gesture as we do through words. Getting up to student teach in front of a bunch of college students helped me discover my inner teacher/entertainer. Simultaneously, I decided to develop a show based on these concepts in a small club located close to campus. That endeavor proved so successful that I eventually took it on the road, performing my mind games for audiences and shortly thereafter sharing my insights about tooling up our minds (and improving our communication and relationship skills) with corporate America.

After doing my doctoral work at NYU, I wanted a job in the most esoteric think-tank environment I could find, and to use my hard-won degree for the betterment of mankind. So naturally I went to *Sesame Street*, where I worked as a director of research for 10 years. During that time, I used my learnings, studies, abilities, and professional training to help determine the best methods for transmitting ideas to kids. Television teaches kids by showing, not telling, a notion that would shape the *Sesame Street* world from simple concepts like the alphabet to complex ideas like community values.

Which gets us, finally, back to this book. We all harbor the kinds of abilities that I've used all my life. The real secret is that just because we're not conscious of absorbing information doesn't mean that it's not there. We just don't know how to listen to it, or we throw it away as nonsense. That's about to change. I'm about to show you, as best I can, how to unlock your hidden mental powers by giving you a variety of ways to become more aware of the details you've been missing, and by illuminating and stretching your mind so that it can process that input.

This critical information can transform your life by making you more effective in everything you do. As a parent, you'll be able to determine what's on your children's minds, their strengths and limitations, as well as whether they're telling you the truth. You'll also learn how best to communicate with them—and that usually doesn't involve words. As a mate, the information you're about to gain about reading, dealing with, and appealing to people will help you relate to each other better. At work, you'll exhibit newfound confidence—to me the most critical component of success—along with your new master mind.

Failed businessman George W. Bush said to James Robinson, "I feel like God wants me to run for president. I can't explain it, but I sense my country is going to need me. Something is going to happen . . . I know it won't be easy on me or my family, but God wants me to do it." We all know where he ended up. He found the destiny he *knew* to be his. You can find yours.

The book is divided into two overlapping yet distinct parts. Part I covers what I call the Hardware Keys: These are the three keys that lay the intellectual and practical foundations of creating a master mind. They are Relaxation, Attention, and Meaning—what I call RAM. It is your basic hardware.

Part II addresses the Software Keys. These keys are a bit softer, dealing as they do with areas that, while practical, at first blush seem not to have the edge of RAM. Suffice it to say that the skills developed in IMP—Intuition, Memory, and Play—are of even greater value than RAM because their application is so vast.

Through the *six keys* you will unlock many secrets and begin on some exciting journeys. You will understand how to tap into this mental jet stream with the help of entertaining exercises that illustrate, clarify, and utilize the principles of each key, and "mindscripts," self-talk approaches to help you to retrain your mind.

The first key will unlock the secrets and functions of RELAXATION; you'll learn your mind's true capacity as well as see how that single key will allow you to open the gates to the rest of your innate mental powers.

The second key—ATTENTION—will teach you how to actually see aspects of your world that your conscious mind currently overlooks, thereby giving you invaluable focus, concentration, and decision-making sensitivity.

Key number 3, which spans Chapters 4, 5, and 6, reveals the secrets of making MEANING, transforming simple sensory input into meaningful situations. This revelation of the meaning of nonverbal communication and other signals are conduits into people's thoughts and give you an invaluable inside track.

This key also unlocks the mysteries in Chapter 4, where you'll learn how to use these nonverbal cues to tell truth from lies, a survival skill today in love, work, even parenting

Finally in Key 3 you will explore the power of INFLUENCE, which will help you to utilize the meaning-making process to impress and influence others in order to improve both your personal and business dealings

Key 4, INTUITION, will show you how to turn on and access your intuition to provide unique insight and problem-solving success.

Key 5, MIND and MEMORY, will help you strengthen your mind muscles through improving your concentration and your memory, both of which will bolster your ability to pick up—and take advantage of—the cues you're learning in this program.

In Key 6, or PLAY, you'll discover that since every thought manifests itself physically, you can play and take intuitive problem-solving a step further by using a pendulum to help answer questions that might otherwise stump you and solve the stickiest of problems. And you'll find the final keys to unlock your master mind, games to help you practice what you've learned, and one last test to check just how far you've come in the development of your mental abilities.

If all this sounds daunting, it's not. Despite the fact that you may not have my natural ability or extensive training, you can still learn to do what I do. I don't read people's deepest, darkest secrets. I read thoughts. There's a difference. A thought is something that you focus on, that comes and goes depending on what you're doing and thinking. I'm not a mind reader, I'm a thought reader. Nothing that I do is supernatural or occult. It's all based on human behavior and human management. The tricks of the psychologist, magician, advertising man, clergy, and comedian are all worthy tools in my quest for mind. I pick up the cues and read *people*: I am a student of the human mind, and I've been one my whole life. I don't do anything that a 10-year-old couldn't do—with 30 years of practice.

PART 1

HARDWARE KEYS— FOUNDATIONS (RAM)

CHAPTER 1

RELAXATION (KEY 1)

EASE ON DOWN THOSE SYNAPSES

This chapter will lay the groundwork that will allow you to unlock the enormous power in your mind. You *can* read thoughts and body language, detect lies, intuit answers, problem-solve, and do wonders you could not imagine. I will teach you how best to access mental powers you don't even know you have. It's said that we use only 10 percent of our minds. I certainly don't know what 100 percent is, but I do know that we only use a fraction of our mental power. The rest just sits there because we don't know how to access it. That's about to change. And that will transform your life.

The first key, you may be surprised to discover, is learning how to relax.

Of course, this doesn't mean that you'll all of a sudden be able to read thoughts, or that you'll be able to take your own show on the road. Anyone can learn the basics of drawing and still not be an artist (actually, considering what's selling out there, maybe you can). And clearly, though most of us know how to write sentences, we wouldn't—and couldn't—write a book if our lives depended on it. Further, we all know that the basic ability to tell jokes does not a stand-up comedian make. So you may not be able to be me. But you can still tap your own mental prowess and make your own mental magic.

> Relaxing your mind is the number one key in unleashing its power . . . and it has power in itself. All other keys start with your mind at rest, with your alertness high, and your stress levels low.

You don't have to leave this up to chance. You can program your mind so that your body, emotions, and perceptions are more finely tuned. I'll show you how to do that through what I call *mindscripts*, or simply self-talk.

When you talk to yourself in a directed way (a mindscript), you are in a state that is conducive to change in yourself. A basic form of biological communication occurs via the release of biochemical transmitters in the body, and a kind of autosuggestion takes place. This is how mindscripts work. You program your mind with the script and other levels of consciousness take over.

By working on the mind and producing changes in it, we can expect the person as a whole to be influenced at many levels. This premise rests at the very core of mindscripts and how they operate. To open the floodgates, however, your conscious mind that's been working overtime needs a break. You have to relax.

You know, stress is part of life. At work or school it can be exams, competition, deadlines, or indecision or relationships. At home it can be finances or interpersonal areas. It is a fact that stress can make you sick . . . and no doubt has negative effects and influence on mind and body.

FIGHT OR FLIGHT

We have two built-in mechanisms to protect our health: the stress response and its antidote, the relaxation response. Our stress response kicks in automatically when we feel threatened. The heart speeds up, breathing becomes faster and shallower, blood pressure rises, and we're ready for "fight or flight."

This survival mechanism is great for short-term emergencies, like being chased by a bear. Your adrenaline rushes and your response is to run like mad, find a hiding place, or go to battle.

But it's harmful when triggered and sustained by anticipated fears. Or in a situation that does not let you fight or flight. If your boss comes down hard on you, chances are you cannot run away, you cannot hide, and, unless looking for a lawsuit, you cannot engage him in battle. This inability to do what your body wants to

---

BASICS OF LEARNING TO RELAX

Many of us who manage our outside lives skillfully are often clueless when it comes to knowing what our own bodies need. We have to learn how to relax. Here are some tips:

1. Observe how your mind and body respond to events (notice when you tense up, when you relax).
2. Make tension-release a habit: Stretch your neck (chin to chest, chin to each shoulder, ear to each shoulder), gaze at the sky, stretch muscles, and take deep breaths any time, anywhere.
3. When under stress, repeat to yourself: "Calm body, clear mind."
4. Take up an activity to balance your life: Try ceramics, a martial art, wrestling, quilting, calligraphy, singing, tae kwon do.
5. Take a hot bath or get a massage.
6. Plan something fun.
7. Watch a TV comedy or funny video.
8. Get absorbed in a game.
9. Have lunch with a friend or go to the movies.
10. While driving, play soothing music.
11. Alternate activities: Do vigorous exercise after concentrated work.

do leads to physiological changes that affect your immune system, sleep, and digestion, and can lead to serious problems.

But when the relaxation response is invoked, heart rate slows, muscles relax, and breathing deepens and slows. Relaxation reduces anxiety, fear, muscle tension, pain, healing time, and sleep problems. It strengthens the immune system and enables you to renew yourself in the midst of continuous change. Furthermore it provides the calm you need to understand your boss's mind and strategize your next move to control him and/or the situation.

RELAXATION TECHNIQUES

Physical Exercise: Whether it's a 65-mile bike ride or a quick walk around the building, exercise is a proven method of releasing muscle tension.

More Relaxation: Tense each group of muscles for 10 seconds and then suddenly release them. Notice the difference.

Meditation: You stop everything to quietly reach a "still point." Here the mind is calm and clearly aware, stress is let go, and both mind and body relax.

Yoga: This discipline involves breathing and holding certain positions.

Mindscripts/Self-talk/Self-hypnosis/Visualization—Imagery (all the same thing): Repetition of positive expressions such as "I will do well." You relax and focus your own mind on a relevant topic. You "see" yourself relaxed, successful, happy, joyful, or whatever rings your chimes.

TOTAL RELAXATION

Let's begin by defining total relaxation. You may feel you are totally relaxed when you have finished a hard day at work, and you come home and seat yourself in your favorite chair. I'm afraid this is not the case. Thoughts of the day are still racing through your mind. Various personal problems keep flashing in and out. Certain fears and anxiet- ies are still foremost in your mind. Muscles remain tense. Perhaps your feet ache or your back hurts. I'll even bet you can't remember when you've gotten a really good night's sleep. Unfortunately, you have not even begun to let all that go. Total relaxation is a state of mind and body, which must be consciously developed and practiced.

This is literally the foundation for everything else that follows in this program. You cannot get in tune if you are stressed and not listening. So whatever you do, don't skip over this part.

To achieve total relaxation, your mind must be tranquil—void of all thoughts. Your muscles must be completely loose. Physical or mental distractions will only impede your progress. If you would like to find out just how tense and unrelaxed you really are, try this simple experiment. Look around you and let your eyes fall on a simple object in the room. Make sure the object is relatively small and not too complex in design. An ashtray or decorator item would be perfect. Gaze at this object for a minute or so, noting its exact design, its color, and other various characteristics. Then, close your eyes and visualize this object in your mind's eye. Be sure the image is bright and clear, the edges are sharp, and the color does not fade. Hold this image for 5 minutes without letting it flicker or weaken. If you have discovered you can't do it, don't be discouraged. Unless a person has developed his ability to relax and concentrate, the best he will be able to do is 10 to 20 seconds.

By mastering total relaxation, in essence, you place yourself into an altered state of consciousness. Your body rates—from breathing to heartbeats—slow. Though you remain fully conscious and aware, you will not hear distractive sounds around you, and you will not see movements, even though others near you may be dis- turbed by these conditions.

It is at this state of concentration that the ability to send and receive thoughts is at its highest. This is the stage you will attempt to achieve. The following mindscript will help you achieve that state of total relaxation—the first step toward unlocking the power of your mind. You'll want to practice this or some of the other relaxation techniques again and again to enhance their effects.

RELAXATION MINDSCRIPTS

Don't worry if you don't achieve a fully tranquil state the first time you try this. Just relax and enjoy!

Total Relaxation Mindscript

To begin, select a room in your home where you can be alone for about 30 minutes a day. Be sure the room is quiet and there are no distractions. The room should be cool and well ventilated, and should be relatively dark, so pull the curtains and turn off the lights. Naturally, you will need to keep your radio, stereo, or television turned off. Wear as much or as little clothing as you feel necessary, but be sure that what you select is loose fitting and not too warm. Remove any jewelry you may be wearing—headbands, curlers, rings, necklaces, watches—anything that could cause a physical distraction. Tight-fitting underclothing, such as shorts, panties, and bras, should also not be worn.

Select a chair that is comfortable, preferably a soft armchair. Elevate your feet with a stool or another chair to prevent the blood from going to your feet. Sit back in the chair, elevate feet, relax, and make yourself comfortable. Allow your body to go limp starting with the legs and moving up to the abdomen, the shoulders, the arms, the neck, and the face. Close your eyes.

All breathing should be done through the nostrils, not the mouth. If, during this exercise, the hair in your nose vibrates, slow down your breathing. You are going to inhale slowly to a count of 10, hold your breath for a count of 3, and then exhale to a count of 10. Repeat this process for a total of 10 times. Keep your eyes closed and begin breathing in a regular manner for a few seconds.

By this time, if you have followed directions properly, you should have attained a state of light relaxation. Your breathing should now be stable and unrestricted, and your muscles should no longer be tense.

Now, contract, or tighten, every muscle in your body. Begin with the left foot. Tighten every muscle in the left foot and hold them tight. Do the same with your right foot. Continue up the body to the muscles in your legs, abdomen, chest, shoulders, arms, hands and fingers, neck, and face. At this point, every muscle in your body should be straining. Hold this tension to a count of 10, then gradually let your body go limp, beginning with the feet and working up the body in exactly the same order. At this stage you should feel every nerve in your entire body relaxing, tingling with a pleasant sensation of lightness.

Enjoy the overall sensation of being totally relaxed. Imagine you are rising; your body is floating on a soothing cushion of warm air. Think of nothing but this sensation. After a few seconds, imagine yourself being lowered to the chair. Slowly open your eyes—look around—familiarize yourself with the serene, pleasant state of relaxation that you have attained. Rest for a few moments before resuming your normal activities.

This relaxation exercise should be performed every day, twice a day if possible. With each session your mind and body will become more responsive. Each time you will be able to relax your mind and body more easily, and the amount of time required to reach total relaxation will diminish. The first few times you attempt this exercise, you may require 20 to 30 minutes to reach total relaxation. Perhaps you will be unable to relax at all the first time you try it. Don't be discouraged if this happens—the more often you practice this exercise, the easier it becomes. Within 2 to 3 weeks you should be able to attain total relaxation in a matter of 1 to 2 minutes.

Relaxation Pick-Me-Up

If you don't have time to do the full relaxation script, try this quick script below any time you need to dissipate stress. Stress, after all, is the kryptonite of clear thinking. Thus relaxation allows your mind to be receptive and clears pathways in your mind that would otherwise be blocked.

Feel all the stress draining away from your left big toe. Drifting and draining away. It is feeling totally, completely, entirely relaxed. All tension is erased; there is only contentment and calm in your big toe. Visualize this relaxation spreading to the other toes on your left foot. It may be a gentle slow spread, or perhaps your big toe can no longer contain its abundance of relaxation and it bursts, flowing into the adjoining toes. Feel the toes becoming fully relaxed. Now, that relaxation is spreading into your left foot, filling it entirely, spreading, and creeping slowly to your ankle and up your leg, your calf muscles, your shin, your knee, up your thigh to the top of your leg. Your whole left leg is fully and completely relaxed. See it in your mind and feel it.

Now focus your attention on your right big toe and repeat the procedure until both legs are fully relaxed. The first time you do this you will be distracted by other thoughts; your mind will be racing. That is totally natural and understandable. As with all skills, it will improve with practice. Even if it is not totally satisfactory the first time, you will see a big difference and it will get better and better each time you complete it. When you are distracted, just smile to yourself because you understand what is happening and then return to the point where you left off.

When your legs are fully relaxed, concentrate on your left thumb, seeing and feeling it becoming relaxed, then the fingers, palm, wrist, forearm, elbow, upper arm, shoulder. Then the same with the right arm. Now feel the relaxation spreading from the top of your legs into your lower stomach, your inner organs, up through your rib cage, upper chest, and shoulders.

Give a little extra time to your neck and shoulders as there is a lot of tension here. Feel the relaxation spreading up your neck, into your jaw, cheeks, past your ears, your eyes, and right up to and over the top of your head. Again feel that power within you. Take a few deep breaths; allow your mind and body to feel calm and relaxed.

When you have mastered total relaxation in the quiet surroundings of your room, and the needed time to achieve it is down to less than a minute, you can progress to the point where you can call upon your abilities to totally relax in any surroundings, even in the busiest and noisiest places. Do what it takes to master this script. This cannot be rushed, and you cannot even hope to develop other scripts until you can totally relax.

Did the mindscript make sense to you or did it seem like nonsense? How successful was it? What did it do for you? Make a mental or physical note of your responses.

You can now continue with your work. If you feel sidetracked at all, close your eyes for just a few moments and feel that power within you radiating throughout your whole body. You can do this last bit as often as you need to during the day, as it takes only a few seconds.

Once you have read through the relaxation mindscript and feel you understand what is required, make it your own talk.

Modify, create, and cultivate your own powerful imagery. Be creative! I once had a student who sought help from me because his overactive mind kept him awake at night. He compared the feeling of racing thoughts in his head to a merry-go-round whirling at high speed. I explained how he could use that very image to calm his thoughts. From then on, whenever he wanted to still his mind, all he did was imagine the merry-go-round with its blurring colors and blaring music, pull out the plug, and watch it gradually slow down until it stopped completely! He found this greatly helped to quiet his mind at the end of each day, allowing him to practice some mindscripts before drifting into a peaceful sleep.

While practicing the mindscripts, make a point of finding the symbolic imagery that works best for you. The exploration itself is part of the discovery. You are in control.

As with any program, actually doing the exercises rather than simply reading along will help you maximize your growing mental powers. Though you'll want to try all the exercises, eventually you'll narrow your repertoire to those that make sense to you, that suit you, and you'll practice those more. And that's exactly what you need to do because no one thing appeals to everyone. Think of this as a cookbook: You choose the recipes that appeal to you, you add ingredients based on your personal experience, and you cook up a dish to your taste.

So let's get started by finding out just how built-up those mental powers already are. Take the following quiz to see where you stand on the master mind fitness scale. Unlike most tests, there are no right or wrong answers. At the end of the program, you'll simply take exactly the same quiz and compare your answers to see how the development of your master mind is coming along.

Six Keys is not just about controlling people's thoughts, it's about using the awesome potential of your mind to connect more deeply to your own feelings, to the people in your life, and to the world around you. When you buy a car, a washing machine, a cell phone, an iPod, or even a houseplant, you usually get an owner's manual. Only our mind, the one device we use and rely upon every second of our lives, comes without instructions and directions.

QUIZ

1. Have you tried recently to get someone to do what you want and did it work?
2. Do you tend to think and observe at a superficial or a profound level? How do you know?
3. Have you been successful at trying to read someone's thoughts?
4. Do you relax easily?
5. Is your stress level low or high?
6. Do you consider yourself a creative person?
7. Are you an imaginative problem-solver?
8. Are you observant when it comes to detail?
9. Do you read people correctly? How do you know?
10. How attuned are you to nonverbal communication?
11. Are you aware of the messages that your body language—and even choice of clothing and accessories—says about you?
12. Have you ever tried to ascertain whether or not a person was lying to you? Were you successful?
13. Have you successfully influenced someone's choice or changed how they thought about an issue?
14. Do you exercise your mind?
15. Can you remember names easily? How about facts and figures?
16. Are you intuitive when it comes to people and events?
17. Have you ever had a precognitive (predictive) experience?
18. Can you sense danger?
19. Do you have a knack for finding misplaced or lost items?
20. Have you ever tried alternative approaches to solving a problem?
21. Do you remember your dreams?
22. Can you use visualization to try to get what you want? Are those efforts effective?
23. On a scale of one to 10, how well do you feel you're using your mind's potential?

Consider, then, the *six keys* as an owner's manual to help you optimize the mechanics of your mind.

The next step in this process? Just stop, look, and listen in a whole new way.

MIND TOOLS

Here's a simple test to see how far you've already come in terms of relaxing. Perform the relaxation mindscript or any of the relaxation techniques already noted in this chapter before going to bed. Then, instead of setting your alarm clock, write down in the chart below the time you wish to awaken. Tell yourself, "I'm going to wake up at 7:00 a.m., I'm going to wake up at 7:00 a.m., and I'm going to wake up at 7:00 a.m." If you have a normal night's sleep, you'll wake up within minutes of the time that you're setting your mind to. We've all done it, but you can do this like clockwork. Or can you? Try it every night this week (though if you've really got to be somewhere, you might want to set a backup alarm just in case).

	Time you scripted yourself to wake up	Time you actually woke up
Day 1		
Day 2		
Day 3		
Day 4		
Day 5		
Day 6		
Day 7		

How did you do? Did you improve over the week? Did the self-talk help reprogram your mind? Stick with it. It will.

MIND-BUILDING TIP

To instinctively become aware of (and thus control) time, just take off your watch. If you're a slave to your timepiece, but not truly aware of time as a tool, this will force you to think and behave differently.

---

8 WAYS TO HAVE A MENTAL CHILL-OUT

We all need to put it away sometimes; just as your body needs a break, so does your mind, and you just can't pack it up and send it to Sandals for the week. Here are some ways to give your mind a mini-vacation, without Prozac or even calling Travelocity.

Play technological hooky: Borrow some computer time from work and go surfing. Just let that Internet highway carry you where it will—games, ladies, diaries, illusions, music, places, it will take you to a world outside yourself where you can mentally shut down. Try it every day at the same time, or, if you can get away with it, a full day (week) of mind-numbing bliss.

Reread a favorite book: No, not a new one, but an old friend. The familiar and the novel will mix quite well and send your mind on a gentle trip down a road you've been before . . . and enjoyed. Even more pleasurable is falling asleep in a favorite chair while reading . . . it's as if the gods put you on a pillow of clouds and blanketed you with spring mist.

The Zen of forbidden fruit: The masters knew that singular concentration brought about bliss. OD on what you love. Dream about it, think about it, if you dare—talk about it, all to excess. You may even do it as long as it isn't detrimental to your health and it's not illegal. Fried food, skinny women, cartoons from the '60s, watching Fox for hours on end, indulging in live sporting events on radio-TV-Internet. The point is to satiate those desires, feel reinvigorated. Then you can go on with life . . . until the next vacation is needed.

The mantra of nothing: Try to think of nothing. At first it may seem impossible, but hey, the federal, state, and local governments do it all the time. You may wish just to think of a nonsense syllable (try "smo" . . . it's my favorite) over and over again, and let nothing else enter your mind. You will feel cleansed after a 10-minute workout.

Manipulate time: Sleep from 4:00 to 8:00 p.m. and you won't miss out on much but will feel that you have a whole evening to play and take that mini-vacation.

Or try spending just a few minutes getting into your office with your eyes closed while doing all the things you normally would do when starting your day. It'll have the same effect on your thrill-seeking endorphins as a bungee jump.

The gravity-free workout: Visualize your body taking up a larger and larger space, until it seems to float (eyes open optional). Do this for about 5 minutes for an air-balloon-like surge of vacation.

Take three fantasy vacations: Take a moment and jot down the ones you would love to take, if money and time were no object!

• Where would you go?

• Who would go with you?

• What would you like to do?

• How long would you like to be away?

• What would you enjoy seeing . . . experiencing . . . discovering?

• What would be the high point of your trip?

Enjoy your fantasy vacations. If you wish, go further and get some information on these places.

• Would you like at least one to come true?

• What steps would be necessary?

I leave the rest up to you—whether you simply daydream or bring about a new reality.

Spend time alone: This may be some of the most comforting and stimulating times of your day.

CHAPTER 2

ATTENTION (KEY 2)

DISCOVER WHAT YOU'VE BEEN MISSING AND SEE WHAT YOU'VE NEVER SEEN BEFORE

By now you're well on your way to mastering the art of relaxing. In order to make the most of the world around you, you need to gain a clearer, more accurate, and complete perception of what you've been missing. By understanding your limitations, you'll raise your consciousness and gain the correct input upon which to base interpersonal interactions.

"You can see a lot just by looking," baseball great Yogi Berra has said. Yogi, in his own inimitable way, knows what he's talking about. The world around you is yours to interpret and to use—just look and see. If you can make sense of what the world is telling you, you can tune your awareness like you would tune a radio, bringing in clearer and clearer signals for your own enjoyment and benefit.

So often, however, we see what we want to see (or not see). Our attention is unfocused. We selectively perceive the world around us, often missing other possibilities that may be staring us in the face. We fall into patterns that hide or confuse those other possibilities. This is the state most of us live in all our lives. It's called selective perception.

Not convinced? Try these deceptively simple perceptual tests.

How many Fs are in the following statement?

FINISHED FILES ARE THE RE-
SULT OF YEARS OF SCIENTI-
FIC STUDY COMBINED WITH THE
EXPERIENCE OF MANY YEARS.

If you counted three, you are wrong. There are six. Because the F in "of" sounds like a V, it seems to disappear. Habit makes us fail to perceive many things, and past-learned patterns create expectations to perceive in a particular way.

A good friend of mine, a sharp-minded CEO of a Fortune 500 company, was pulled over for running a stop sign. He had been relocated to another country for a while, and the sign had been put up during his absence. He got used to driving down that street without stopping, and because of that mental pattern, he did not realize that there was a stop sign. By the way, he paid his fine—pleading faulty perceptual expectation just doesn't hack it in the eyes of the law.

Most of us stumble through life shielded, cocooned, half-blinded, and unaware of the new and exciting world around us every second. Inattention can lead to danger. Even as a kid, I knew this, though I probably wouldn't have put it like that. I would have said, "Don't go that way, there are snakes." Which is what I said to my brother when he wanted to go down the Beachwood ravine and I didn't. I didn't know exactly *why* I thought there were snakes—my brother, by this time, knew me well enough to believe me and ventured no farther. Later we found out that the area was literally infested with the varmints. When I thought more about it, I realized that I had picked up on the visual cue of tiny holes in the banks of the ravine, holes that were indeed snakes' homes. It wasn't a conscious connection, but rather my attention looking out for signals. My radar antenna was way up then, and it's way up now. I pay attention, and

I see more than most people. You can learn to do that, too.

Past experience and past learning create our perceptual set. In order to fully experience the powers of your mind, you need to break out of your mind-set and expand your possibilities for perception.

Have you ever purchased a cell phone only to find that the whole world suddenly seems to be using the same phone . . . and same darn ring tone? Don't worry, you're not going crazy. And it's not that sales of these phones dramatically increased overnight, so don't kick yourself for not investing in the company's stock along with its product. Your purchase simply cued you to notice this type of phone, which is now familiar to you. That phone has always been out there, but you now see it differently. Further, you were unconsciously looking for it in an attempt to reinforce your buying decision.

> In order to fully experience the powers of your mind, you need to break out of your mind-set and expand your possibilities for perception.

Some information we perceive and act on, some we do not perceive at all, and some we perceive but ignore. But much of it still enters our mind and has impact; witness what is called the Cocktail Party Phenomenon. Quickly into the first drink, the chatter at lively gatherings hits such a pitch that you can only vaguely hear people talking behind you without really identifying anything they are saying. Until they mention your name, that is. You will usually hear your name distinctly, even once the party hits third cocktail decibel levels. That word will stand out because you are familiar with it.

A while ago I was invited to a cocktail party at the home of a well-known East Side novelist/socialite. Among the guests were Helen Gurley Brown, Gregory Peck, Kurt Vonnegut, and Carl Bernstein. I spent some time demonstrating to this group how thoughts could be guided and "read." We played the hide-an-object game, which you'll find in the last chapter, where I had to find something hidden, using only the tiny nonverbal and unintentional cues given off by the hider. After locating the concealed item, I was challenged to guess Gregory Peck's favorite snack. Much to his astonishment, I did. (If you must know, it's Ritz crackers.)

Then I decided to demonstrate an aspect of the Cocktail Party Phenomenon mentioned above to my elite group, which by now included our hostess. Instead of just listening out for their own names, however, I had them focus their attention (i.e., eavesdrop) on two women having a conversation across the noisy room. See, when you quit talking and focus on others in the room, your mind and attention will be able to distinguish the various conversations. It turned out that the couple under scrutiny was chatting about our hostess, and not in a positive way. We all became a tad embarrassed. Thankfully, she managed to laugh about it. "You know, Marc, I always got bad vibes from those folks but it was just a vague feeling." She continued, "Maybe it's because they talk about me behind my back when I'm around." "And your unconscious picks up on it," I added. Well, it doesn't take a thought reader to figure out which "good friends" won't get invited to the next soiree.

How does this Cocktail Party Phenomenon work? With so much information bombarding our brain, much has to be ignored by our conscious mind. This information isn't really lost; it is merely routed to the unconscious. Awareness of the process is the best way to access it. And access to this information gives you a whole new way to evaluate situations and relationships.

We rely on our senses to tell us what is going on. We see things, people, and situations. We hear noises and words. We taste food and drink. We smell odors and scents. We feel smooth and rough, cool, wet, and slick. Biologically we get input and are stimulated. However, when we perceive something—a sound, a taste, a touch, a sight—what is recorded in our brain is not real. Your mind and experience are constantly re-creating a reality, making meaning out of the experience.

OUR EXPECTATIONS AND HOW OUR MIND CREATES A REALITY

I remember a time when, at a dinner party, I pointed to a white disc of creamy white and brown and asked the waiter, "Cheese?" He nodded yes and I took a slice, expecting the sweet smoothness of a cheesecake to fill my mouth. It was the most vile thing I ever tasted. It turns out it was Brie. Now Brie is not bad, but if your mental expectation is cheesecake, well, you get the picture. We see, hear, and believe what we want to believe, often with limited information and with blinders on. We let experience or expectation fill in the rest of the picture.

TWO DOT EXPECTATION

●   ●

Hold the page about 1 foot from your face. Close or cover your left eye and stare at the dot on the left. You should see them both. Now slowly move the page toward your face. At some point the dot on the right will vanish. Stop moving the page. The dot is gone. Kaput. Now continue to move the page closer . . . the dot returns. Where did it go? Frankly we are all built with a blind spot where the optic nerve connects to the retina; there are no sensory receptors there. We live our lives with a large chunk missing from both sides of our visual field, but our mind fills in the picture. The mind does an amazing thing. It fills in the space with things around it so you can function. You expect a wide field of unbroken vision . . . your mind supplies it.

We are *not* merely passive receivers of all the stimulation "out there," simply because there is no "out there" without our perception of it.

To put it another way, what is out there is so infinitely vast and varied that we must impose order (even if it is artificial) on what's out there to be able to take it in.

> We live our lives with a large chunk missing from both sides of our visual field, but our mind fills in the picture. This is not limited to the visual.

Notice I didn't say "to take it *all* in." We are bombarded by sensations and surrounded by things, people, odors, tastes, happenings, noises, lights, and colors. And that's just the start. It is making order out of the sensory jumble, what William James called life's "buzzing blooming confusion" that is our life's work.

Radio waves, light waves, and electromagnetic waves are omnipresent in this media age where cell phones, infrared, and Bluetooth connections have become routine. If we saw and heard all that was going on around us, we would be so overwhelmed we would be unable to function. So we screen, we choose, we reduce and make meaning out of the "out there."

Regardless of whether you register them, these objects and people that make up the world are not separate from you. Perception is not something that happens to you. You are not a nonparticipating, zombielike recipient of unselected stimulation. You are the force in your own perceptual process, an active partner in what is happening around you. You create your own reality through your perception every second of every day.

We've all looked at strangers and tried to understand who they are, what they do, and what they feel. It is unlikely, however, that two people walking by the same stranger will see that stranger with the same characteristics. In fact one person may not even see the stranger at all.

One of the most amazing social science experiments demonstrates that once an expectation is set, even if it isn't accurate, we tend to act in ways that are consistent with that expectation. Surprisingly often, the result is that the expectation, as if by magic, comes true. Told that a child will turn bad . . . he often does. If our expectation is that those who follow a certain creed are evil . . . we act that way, and they respond similarly to our treatment. The seminal work *Pygmalion in the Classroom* lays it all out.

Schoolteachers were led to believe that certain students selected at random were likely to be showing signs of a spurt in intellectual growth. At the end of the year, the students of whom the teachers had these expectations showed significantly greater gains in intellectual growth than did those in the control group. The group of whom more was expected did significantly better.

Why? Because of expectation and an element of self-fulfilling prophecy. The expectation of the teacher may have created subtle differences in ways the group was treated. Perhaps more reassurance, more praise, more silent approval. The point is they changed. The methodology has been demonstrated time and time again, from small groups learning a factory technique like welding, to massive office settings where clear and timely spreadsheets had to be generated.

We do not perceive things as they are but rather we perceive and create our sense of the world through personal filters. While biologically perception begins with our five familiar senses, there is far more that we draw upon as we construct the reality around us. Our picture of the world depends upon the complex patterns of our past experiences, past knowledge, and the emotional luggage (good and bad) that we carry.

People are more likely to pay attention to those aspects of their environment that they expect or that reinforce what they already know or believe. And people tend to expect or anticipate what they are familiar with.

Familiarity doesn't just breed contempt; it can blind you as well. Read each of the following:

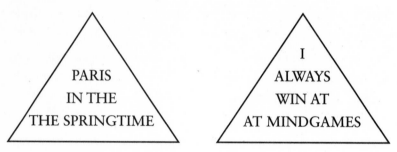

If you caught the extra word in each triangle, give yourself a pat on the back.

F-O-L-K spells _____

P-O-L-K spells _____

The white of an egg is called the _____

I suspect patterning has given you the wrong answer.

The white of an egg is called the albumen.

Are the following correct—yes or no?

$2 + 2 = 4$ $10 + 3 = 1$

$4 + 4 = 8$ $2 + 3 = 5$

$5 + 4 = 9$ $11 + 5 = 4$

The answer is yes to all of them, if you think in terms of time. For example if it is 10:00 a.m. and you add 3 hours, it will be 1:00 p.m.

If you failed in any of these, it may be because your attitude set limited the way you viewed the problem, which limits your ability to problem-solve.

But no more. From now on, when shown a half-filled glass of water and asked if it is half empty or half full, I want you to say that it is completely full. It's just that the glass is too big.

Next, try to wrap your mind around this.

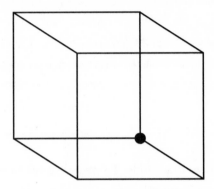

Look at the dot. Is it located in the lower left rear or in the lower left front? We are conditioned to think that squares do certain things—your brain can't process the two things (in this case the front and rear) at the same time. You see either one or the other, not both at the same time.

Your training has a great deal to do with what you perceive. Education, learning, and reading are processes that are vital to perceiving more and taking control of your perceptions: The more you know, the more you perceive. What to the untrained eye, ear, touch, or nose seems the same is full of significant difference to the well-informed.

What is background and what is foreground is not only the basis of optical illusions but is also a building block of our sense of reality and social being. It is not seeing the forest for the trees.

This is of course most obvious with the specialist. A physician will notice the difference between two seemingly identical symptoms. My wife, Tova, is a jewelry designer and artist. She has the ability to distinguish between what to the untrained eye are two

---

MIND BUILDER

You need not be a specialist but merely willing to learn and open your mind. The following exercises are good for building your perception "muscle." Just like building your biceps, your perception muscle will tone up if you exercise it regularly and frequently. Each day observe and study one object closely. Later in the day visualize this object and write down a detailed description. Similarly, observe your own actions and the surrounding world more closely. Form mental images of these actions and objects.

---

seemingly identical diamonds. To me, all gems look alike. I don't know an oval cut from a hexagon cut. They're just sparkly little things to me, and therefore they all look the same. But to an eye that has knowledge of that, they see something very different. If I walk through Central Park with a botanist, we will see two different parks. Communication theory tells us that we don't recognize things until we give them names. Once somebody names something, they will categorize it. If you don't have a name for something, it is just another leaf. By labeling things, we now have ways of categorizing and using it. So, a botanist sees the park differently because it's a world he has labeled, given names to, and now understands. If I question him about what he sees and how he sees it, my world and my perceptions are similarly expanded, and I will begin to see the park as he does.

As you learn new things, you will literally see in a new way. Attention changes perception.

NOW SEE THIS MINDSCRIPT

This mindscript will help enhance your observational abilities.

Close your eyes and allow yourself to enter the total relaxed state.

Visualize your brain as a sponge, absorbing and processing all that you wish to attend to.

See your eyes as powerful telescopes focusing in on the full environment around you.

Tell yourself that your powers of observation will be sharper and clearer.

Notice that your mind tingles in anticipation of the new way that you will see.

Reinforce this feeling of relaxation (remember that?) using imagery and suggestions of your own choosing before bringing this exercise to an end.

Other imagery that may work for you involves imagining your eyes as a movie or video camera, and your mind the screen upon which you project images.

Building and exercising your perceptual abilities is one way to force some organization into that jam-packed chaotic brain of yours. You have to learn how to widen your field of vision and listen with all your senses in order to tap into the power of your mind. Increasing your awareness involves taking off your mental blinders. Selective attention severely limits you reaching full observatory potential. Indeed, most of us confine our minds to what we think we need to know, and don't even know what is right under our noses.

Building and exercising your perceptual abilities is one way to force some organization into that jam-packed chaotic brain of yours.

Let me demonstrate. Imagine a penny, a 1-cent piece, in your mind. You have handled one thousands of times. Now, which way does Lincoln's profile face? Now take one out of your pocket and have a look. Chances are pretty good that you were wrong. Don't worry, most people are. What do you think is in the center of the back of a 1-dollar bill? You've given and received one even more frequently than those annoying pennies. Now, what's on the back? No, it's not an eye and a pyramid. Take a look; you'll be somewhat surprised to see that it is one word. Yes, one.

The secret of using ATTENTION as a powerful KEY tool is to train yourself to see with new eyes every day. Just as you can enhance your physical health with regular exercise,

The secret of using ATTENTION as a powerful KEY tool is to train yourself to see with new eyes every day.

so can you sharpen your powers of attention and observation. By seeing, hearing, and even tasting or smelling what's really perceived as there, you'll be able to base your decisions on fact rather than bias or mistaken assumptions. Sherlock Holmes wasn't psychic, but he sure seemed to be.

How does all this work? Briefly stated, you select your perceptions from what your senses pick up from the environment. You then organize this information into some kind of understandable order *to you*. Finally, you interpret what you have sensed in relation to its context and your past experiences of what you know and believe.

Let us say that you enter a room. You smell something. That's your selective honing of your environment. You categorize it as perfume. That's organizing. You take that to mean that a woman has been in the room. That's interpretation. Of course you may be wrong, depending both on your own experiences and where you are. Men's fragrances are certainly used in many places, and rotting food often first takes on a sweet smell that mimics some perfumes.

Whatever your senses take in means nothing until you've attended to that input. The following exercises will help you identify how you see the world and how your senses are influenced by internal and external factors. This will come in handy every time you make a decision since you'll recognize your own observational tendencies and not be unduly influenced by them.

Make a list of how different moods and environments change your attitude and perceptions. When you are sad, does the living room look the same as when you are happy? When you are angry? How do those emotions affect your experience of music, or noise, or fragrances and odors, or memories?

If you found an object that you've never seen before, how would you go about making meaning of it? What senses do you use? What process do you follow? Notice how you group things, how you create patterns out of what your attention gives you.

If a policeman came to your door, what is your immediate emotional response? Why?

Think of an event (movie, concert, play) that evoked a very different response in you than in the person you went with. What caused the difference?

How many squares do you see? Give it to a friend, how many do they see? How do you explain the differences?

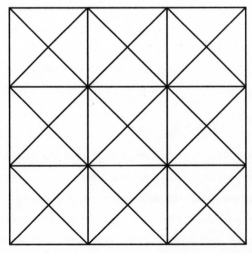

The answer is 26.

A seemingly unsteady man in threadbare clothing comes up to you and says he lost his wallet. Could you lend him $10? He says he'll take your name and address and send the money back to you. What do you do? What if a woman approached you with the same request? Does clothing make a difference?

> Even in social realities our perception of events is colored by expectation or false assumptions.

TRY THIS

There is a cabin on the side of a mountain. Three people are inside and they are dead. How did they die?

Answer: They were killed in a plane crash. The three people were the pilot, copilot, and navigator. They crashed in a snowstorm.

False assumption based on expectations: That the cabin was a mountain cabin. It was actually the cabin of a jetliner.

OR THIS

A man and his son were rock climbing on a particularly dangerous mountain when they slipped and fell. The man was killed, but the son lived and was rushed to a hospital. The old surgeon looked at the young man and declared, "I can't operate on this boy; he is my son." How can this be?

Answer: The old surgeon was the boy's mother.

False assumption: Women aren't surgeons.

TRANSLATION, PLEASE

Once you have your experiences, you have to turn all that data into MEANING, our next KEY.

Based on your past perceptions, expectations, and knowledge, you translate, or make meaning out of experience. The more you expose yourself to the world, the larger your storehouse of information from which to make meaning. The average person walking down a city street may notice (attention) a shadow following him,

MIND BUILDER

Close your eyes and imagine a favorite object. Imagine it clearly in your mind's eye. Now in your mind try the following activities:

- Slowly spin it in front of you
- Examine it from above
- Examine it from below
- Change its color
- Change its color again
- Turn it inside out
- Move it away into the distance
- Make it float
- Magnify it
- Make it tiny
- Make it tinier
- Make it disappear

These mental games will force you to see both how you perceive reality and to consider why. Both the recognition and analysis of your responses will strengthen your observational, interpretational, creative, and intuitive muscles. These exercises help you work more efficiently with your mind to harness the power within it. Now that I've got your attention (get it?), let's jump to translation.

but he won't take the time to focus on it or translate it in any way. He's a sitting duck. With your superior knowledge and experience, your brain sees the shadow, focuses on it, and realizes that the shadow could be any number of things, many of which are dangerous. So maybe you run, maybe you turn around and acknowledge the harmless person walking behind you, but in any case your experience is what tells you that a shadow could potentially be dangerous. You can call it street smarts, but whatever the label, it is a result of your heightened awareness. (Animals often are hardwired to be afraid of certain shadows.)

MIND BUILDER

You can expand your own view of the world around you by seeing your environment through the eyes of a young child. Then try a dog, a bird, or rocks.

We don't always "make meaning" out of what's around us—we have all experienced the feeling of reading the same page over and over again and not really understanding a word. We've paid attention, we know those are letters and that they mean words, but sometimes we're too distracted to make the words connect or mean anything. In that same vein, there is no way you can make meaning out of everything. You'd be exhausted! Your mind automatically shuts out or filters stimuli so that you don't have to translate data every moment of every day. You need to actively choose to translate more of your experience in order to make the most of your mental powers.

Meaning-making is a both a rational and a creative process. Creativity is not something some of us have and others don't. We all have it to be unleashed. Visualization, exploration, curiosity, and fearlessness are all the tools you need. Luckily, you have those in abundance, no matter how buried they might be.

You're also just pages away from learning a new language that you've probably been ignoring even though you're using it every single day.

First, a MIND TOOL to discover how sensitive you have become to the data stream that flows your way and is almost imperceptible to others.

FINGER FEELIES

This test requires two people. Designate one person as the sender, the other as the receiver. The sender places his hand straight out, palm up, fingers spread wide. The sender begins to concentrate on one finger. Direct all your focus to one finger.

The receiver takes his index finger and slowly begins to tap each finger on the sender's outstretched hand. Tap one lightly, then tap the next one and the next. If you wish, you can tap each one more than once. The receiver is trying to get a sense of which finger is being thought of.

Don't make a conscious effort, just relax your mind. One of the fingers you tap will "feel" different. It may feel lighter than the others, or heavier. When you sense that one feels different than the others, point to that finger and have the sender tell you if you were correct or not.

Try it at least 10 times in a row. If you correctly divined the finger two to three times, that's about average. Anything above that is exceptional. After 10 times, switch roles.

Map your results here:

	Correct	Incorrect
1		
2		
3		
4		
5		
6		
7		
8		
9		
10		

CHAPTER 3

MAKE MEANING (KEY 3)—IT'S JUST LIKE MIND READING

LISTEN IN ON THE NONVERBAL WORLD & COMMUNICATE WITHOUT SPEAKING

Our senses know far more—understand far more—than we can easily articulate. Nonverbal language speaks louder than words. It is time you learn how to understand this silent language. Yes, you heard me correctly. "Listening to the voice in your head" does not mean you're nuts, either. It means that you're learning to hear and notice what the world around you is trying to tell you.

The range of nonverbal information is impressive. You can find entire volumes devoted to any one of the kinds of nonverbal communication used daily—books entirely on facial expression; books dealing only with gestures, or spatial relations. In this chapter, I will briefly focus on the basics as they reflect on reading the thoughts of others. To be aware is to have knowledge. This is my mantra.

The point is that language is concerned with the expression of thoughts, ideas, and feelings, and its function is to make communication possible. No one said (or even gestured) that those messages have to be in the form of words. Providing that we understand the message and grasp the meaning of what is being conveyed, words are often unnecessary. Just think of the last time you annoyed the guy in the car behind you. I'm sure he managed to express his anger with just one simple gesture. Of course, not all nonverbal communication is that direct. But it can be just as obvious.

Nonverbal language—which includes tone of voice, eye movements, and use of the physical environment—can communicate what we think, how we feel, and what we want. How? Through physical posture, gestures, facial expression, tone and strength of voice, nonverbal sounds, and space. Because we use this language primarily subconsciously in our dealings with others, we tend to downplay it. That's a mistake. The fact that it is subconscious lets it carry more veracity than the spoken word.

The KEY is to learn how to control your own body language to your advantage and to read others' body language so you know how to react to them appropriately and favorably impact their actions and reactions. That's the best way to make relationships with friends, mates, kids, or work colleagues.

I am constantly amazed that in school we learn the three Rs— reading, writing, and 'rithmetic—but the one mode of information from which we learn about the world most of the time is rarely if ever taught: what anthropologist Edward Hall called the Silent Language. It is the world of the nonverbal.

Though we may not be aware of it, much of our nonverbal behavior is taught to us from the time we are born, and we spend years developing skills that enable us to interpret other people's intentions, meanings, and motives. Most of us take this learning process for granted, so we tend to forget that much of what happens interpersonally actually takes place at this semiconscious level.

When you really think about it, words don't mean much. Not only do they wind up being far less expressive than our actual thoughts, but they often fall short when it comes to conveying meaning. Worse, because they're easily controlled, they're often used to misinform. "I'll have the report ready for you later" sounds like it means something but is full of ambiguity. Just when is "later" . . . today . . . tomorrow . . . after Armageddon? Physical responses help fill in the picture—are they avoiding your gaze, suddenly lowering their voice, pursing their lips . . . certainly red flags that demand you must ask for specifics. Of course the ambiguity on management's part may also play a role: Was there a lack of urgency in the voice or specificity in the request when the assignment was given? The nonverbal element reinforces and at times overrides the spoken word.

Would it surprise you to learn that as little as 7 percent of the messages we communicate face-to-face occur through the words we use? If I told you that voice—pitch, tone, and rhythm—can account for nearly 40 percent of the message conveyed, and posture, gesture, and even scent constitute a

> **So much meaning lies outside of words.**

whopping 50 percent, would you believe me? Well, according to the findings of research into body language, all that is true.

So much meaning lies outside of words, I sometimes think it's a miracle that we manage to be understood by anyone at all. Imagine, however, that instead of limping along on this path to communication and relying on what we're told, as most of us do, we were able to increase our powers of observation to better understand the people and situations around us. We must understand the foundations of the silent language we use all the time in order to expand our perception of the reality around us.

Human beings have limitless potential for thought, focus, and truly astonishing feats of mental control. You can learn how to interpret voice, gesture, and patterns, as well as people's responses to you, and to "read thoughts" by making yourself receptive to other people's impressions and intuitions. We really are in a web of

MIND BUILDER

Try it for yourself by finding a partner and having her put four pieces of paper, one of which she's marked with an X, face down on a table. Have her hold your wrist and think of the one with the X. The held hands are moved, by you, over the four pieces of paper, while the first person thinks of the X.

You have to focus and pay attention to the way the hand is guiding you. The person who knows where the X is will not be aware that she is subtly guiding you, but she will indeed be guiding you. You will feel minute pulls in the direction of the X. Whatever impulses you get to pick a particular piece of paper, say, "This is the one I think has the X." See if you're right.

You may be surprised to find that your partner almost literally pushes your hand in the direction of the hidden X, even though she'll deny she's doing that. That's part of you working with someone else's mind. You're reading a thought.

life, and what affects one person can cause a response in someone else. We're all connected. In the altered state of mind that I will show you how to achieve, you will be more receptive to the tiny tugs on that web that signal meanings that you have never imagined.

The implication that thoughts have physical manifestations is contrary to the way in which you were taught to communicate and understand. The fact that you can pick up on the subtlest of movements that mean something is a new way of seeing the world. A dipped chin as one is talking to you often means subordinance. These people may be quite easily guided by you. On the other hand a straight spine and upped chin may mean you have your work cut out for you in your attempts to influence the person (though, as we will see, there are ways).

A MIND TOOL TO AID IN PICKING UP NONVERBALS

Imagine a world where everyone is sensitive to the thoughts of everyone else. It's not science fiction. Other people and their thoughts are around you all the time, and whether you're aware of it or not, you already pick up on many of these cues. The tools and techniques you're learning in this program will help you tune into these other worlds that surround us. Just like a radio picks up radio waves and turns them into sounds, you can train yourself to tune in to other people's frequency and hear their music. With these tools, we have the power to control and change our world.

This visualization will help enhance your awareness of the non-verbal environment.

Close your eyes and allow yourself to enter the total relaxed state.

Visualize a cylinder or tube coming out of the top of your head and going around the entire room, sucking in everything from the room—the sights, smells, sounds, feelings, even sensations.

Imagine all those now becoming an extension of your mind and your spinal column.

Pull them all in. See the sights, smell the smells, listen to the sounds, feel the feelings, sense the sensations.

Tell yourself that your consciousness and interpretation of elements in the environment will be hyperalert.

See yourself becoming supersensitive to your surroundings.

When you feel "full," shrink your consciousness back into your body.

Explore the environment with enhanced senses.

Aside from exponentially increasing your understanding of people and their actions, nonverbal communication constitutes the basis for reading other people's thoughts. Through it you can see beyond what they say and understand what they mean. I'm not talking about the supernatural, or mind reading, but rather what I call thought reading—those impressions that people give off and that can be translated and guided. When someone slowly nods his or her head up and down, you can be reading a thought. A slow nod usually is a way of their saying "go on" or "I am not interested in taking the speaking role." A rapid up and down may mean "hurry up . . . I've got things to say" or "I wanna get outta here." A smile, a twitch, even a certain fragrance all communicate information.

In my presentations I often will tell the audience to "lift your hand above your head, like this" and will demonstrate. Most will then lift their hands. I then say, looking at my watch, "When I say NOW, I want you to put your hand down." I then go "5, 4, 3, 2, 1" and put my hand down. Ninety percent of the audience will then put their hand down, even though I did not say NOW. It is the power of the nonverbal, expectation of what we infer rather than what is said, that carries the most weight.

You can use knowledge about nonverbal communication to figure out when someone's words belie their thoughts or emotions. I collect books, first editions. I went book shopping at an antiques store where I found a nice first edition of a book I wanted to buy. All well and good. I asked the man behind the counter the price of the book, and he gripped the counter, stared me straight in the eyes, unblinking, and said, "$150." I think you can see where I'm going with this. He wasn't meaning to tell me that he was trying to dominate me through his stare with the number he was giving me, but to me it was obvious he was trying to overprice. Now I'm not a bargainer, I don't enjoy haggling with merchants, but I went right up to this guy and said, "It's not worth more than $50," and turned to leave. Suffice it to say, I bought it for $50.

The "language" of nonverbal communication is a whole system in itself, one that can be actively used. With a little practice, you can tell when someone's nonverbal cues contradict rather than reinforce what their mouth is saying. Keep in mind, too, that nonverbal cues to a large extent can't be controlled by the people exhibiting them. This gives the reader of these cues a huge advantage over the hapless subject, who is exhibiting his real meaning behind everything he says. All you have to be is attuned to picking up those nonverbal cues that we routinely take for granted and ignore.

Next time a salesman's badgering you, here's how to uncover his true intentions. First, understand that on a shelf of five DVD players, say, the high-markup items will be displayed second from the left and second from the right at eye level. (Statistically, consumers don't purchase from the edges or middle as often.) If he's pushing one of these products, ask, "Is this the one you'd buy?" Now watch his eyes. If his pupils grow larger or if he averts his gaze, you've struck a nerve. Not only is his mood changing, you're seeing his internal truth emerge. And no matter what he actually says, you have your answer—it's not.

Even if you never learned to count to five in French or never got the hang of pig Latin, you can learn this nonverbal lingo. In fact, I would go so far as to say you already know it, you just don't know that you know it.

HOW WE THINK ALWAYS
SHOWS SOMEWHERE

If thinking processes are reflected in the way we use our physical environment, they probably manifest themselves in other forms of nonverbal behavior as well. The body and mind are inseparable. How we think always shows somewhere, if you know where to look. In particular, it shows in breathing patterns, skin color, and posture. Think about the last time you asked your spouse or a very close friend how he was, and he said in a dead voice, "Fine." You know he's not fine, quite the opposite. And you know that because of the way his face didn't reflect what "fine" looks like, and his voice didn't denote what "fine" sounds like. You can recognize false cheer when you see it, often without knowing how you know it to be false. What about after a date? Does the guy mean it when he says, "I'll call you," or is that a polite way of saying, "I'm never going to call you as long as I live"? You can usually tell the difference—body language, in all its many forms and manifestations, is working to communicate what the speaker is really saying. Though we often deny what we know to be real.

A person cannot _not_ communicate. This is a basic tenet of nonverbal language. We are always communicating, giving off signals and information.

Our handwriting, too, can convey messages other than the words we're writing: Downward sloping lines across a page indicate a less-than-cheerful outlook, while open, loopy writing and flourishes show the opposite.

Even on a crowded bus, we're giving off those don't-talk-to-me signals: lowered eyes, head turned away, gaze fixed and unfocused. By deliberately _not_ communicating, we're communicating that we don't want to communicate right now.

SMILE, YOU'RE ON NONVERBAL CAMERA

Facial expressions convey a wealth of information about how a person feels, what she thinks, and what she is trying to—and not trying to—say. Practice your face reading on total strangers. Look at faces you pass on the street. What do they bring to mind? If you described each one in a single word, would you say happy? Sad? Bored? Disinterested?

Study the faces. What are the differences between them? Why does each one seem to be expressing what you describe?

Now hone in on the most obvious displayer of meaning: the smile. Smiles come in all shapes and guises. Everyone smiles when happy, even those people who are blind, deaf, and unable to speak, so smiling is not something we learn to do: It is innate. There are really three kinds of smiles—the real smile, the unhappy smile, and the false smile. It is a fact of life that smiles can be used to try to hide behind, as in the case of someone who smiles through adversity, disappointment, or loss, and likewise, there are people who seem able to smile and hold pleasant conversations with those they find difficult or whom they dislike. People who work with the public, in the service industries, or who perform in public, like me, are well used to smiling when they may not personally feel the inclination to do so. Consequently we should always bear in mind that a smile may be, well, less than genuine. Knowing how to distinguish—and interpret—the real thing from the fake can be as important as knowing the difference between a genuine diamond and rhinestones.

The real smile is the felt smile—the sort of smile that scrunches up our eyes, opens our mouth a little, and shows our teeth. It is slow to come and fades slowly. The simple smile, often seen when people are smiling to themselves over a private thought, is a cut-down version of the felt smile.

The unhappy smile is worn when we are trying to put on a brave face. Often the corners of the mouth are pulled sideways rather than up. The eyes usually have no joy and no scrunching. While we are trying to tell everyone around us that we are fine, in fact we are probably unhappy about something, or even insecure, and seeking to avoid showing our true feelings, which would lead to questions we would prefer to avoid.

False smiles, familiar to anyone who's ever been lied to (which means all of us), last longer than genuine smiles but come on suddenly and fade just as rapidly. They are held in place, the lips are stiff and stretched, and the eyes will stay unsmiling, with no cheerful crinkling at the corners.

When we meet friends, our smile varies slightly. We can smile showing our top teeth only. The broad smile shows both sets of teeth and the grin is open and wide. This is the sort of smile that often turns into laughter, and someone who smiles like this a lot is likely to be an extrovert. (Laughter itself, like smiling, is quite individual, with people often being recognized by their laugh, even when miles—or an ocean—away from home.)

HERE'S LOOKING AT YOU

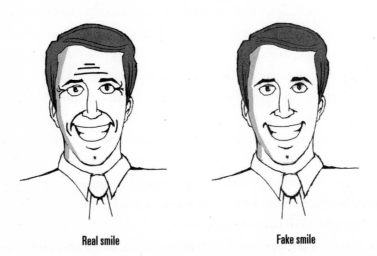

Real smile   Fake smile

Learning to read someone's expressions, mannerisms, and communication patterns correctly can be downright profitable. If someone you're standing face-to-face with stares you right in the eye and says, "That is my final offer," he doesn't mean it. We just don't communicate that way. He's trying to be overly emphatic, and that's a cue that he doesn't mean what he says. On the flip side, you can use your own knowledge about nonverbal nuance when negotiating. My wife, Tova, considers haggling part of the charm of foreign (and even some domestic) bargaining, be it in the *shuk*, the *mercado,* or the local flea market. When the supposedly final price is given, she turns her back and starts to walk away. Nine times out of 10, they call her back and finally make her that offer she can't refuse. She uses her intuition, as well as her body language smarts, to ascertain just how far she can push.

You can become a professional-grade observer of facial and body language all around you—an observer extraordinaire, if you will. For starters, watch people while they're talking. Practice studying people in conversation everywhere—at work, at a party, in a restaurant, on a plane, or in the park. Look for all the variations possible in different mannerisms or silent signals. You may even experiment watching television with the sound off (actually not a bad idea to do all the time).

The next time you're out shopping for something that the salesman has to sell you, really scrutinize his body language. How many kinds of smiles do you see, and how would you evaluate them? How about frowns, smirks, finger pointing, dry coughs, and toe tapping? You must put in the work of noticing and cataloging every tic, every movement, every idiosyncrasy. Does the computer salesperson appear confident about his merchandise? Does he appear overly glib? Does his pitch convey any doubts? If he's good, it won't. He wants to send out only the signals that will make you buy. Observe mannerisms and try to assess the situation. What is he doing and why?

Soon you will become a collector of mannerisms. The habit of putting the overt behavior of others under the scrutiny of your own private magnifying glass is not only easy but also considerably entertaining. Besides, it will make you more sensitive to those around you.

Several well-known criminal lawyers have developed this skill for use in situations where even the slightest edge gives them an advantage. Police, therapists, teachers, clergy, and CEOs of the Fortune 500 have all attended my programs, often with the specific purpose of sensitizing themselves to the actions of others. For all these occupations, paying attention to patterns of communication, seeing what doesn't fit, and being able to read between the lines and elicit information can mean the difference between success and failure. And while that's important for all of us, it's life and death for some.

In this age of terrorism, security demands that those responsible for protecting the public know how to spot behaviors that indicate potential threats. The ability to identify inappropriate or "out-of-place" body language in others enables security personnel to respond quickly to complex situations and to distinguish between those that carry a threat and those that do not. It all gets back to context. For example, the panic engendered by a mother losing sight of her child in a public place would not be interpreted as threatening, even though the body language of those involved might indicate high levels of anxiety and stress.

During one training course a female airport security officer reported that she had apprehended a woman who was carrying drugs strapped to her body. The woman looked pregnant but, according to the security officer, her suspicions were aroused because the suspect didn't have a pregnant face. Such sensitivity to detail (the language of the body) has much to do with intuition, or having an "experienced eye for the unexpected."

Actors and politicians (often unfortunately one and the same) have also taken advantage of the knowledge of nonverbal communication. President George W. Bush, for example, exudes warmth in a way that his adversary in the 2004 elections simply didn't. In addition to his "aw shucks" self-deprecating manner, which makes him seem so accessible, he uses touch to cement his bonds with those he's talking to. With training, John Kerry could have learned to overcome the chilly New England formality that he exuded during the campaign and been able to display similar amiability.

But it's not just a question of what you put out but also what you take in. By developing your innate ability to read faces and body language, you increase your ability to influence others as well.

How many variations can you observe of each signal listed below?

Facial Expressions

breaking eye contact	smile
closing eyes	smirk
face losing color	sneer
frown	squint
grinding teeth	stare
laugh	startled look
open mouth	tight lips
raised eyebrows	wetting lips
rapid blinking	worried look

Gestures

covering eyes	rubbing face
covering mouth	rubbing nose
cracking knuckles	scratching head
hand wave	steeple gesture
head shake	showing palms

making fist

nodding

picking lint

pointing finger

tapping fingers

touch

twisting ring

wringing hands

Body Display

arm folding

body slumping

dry cough

head bowing down

head turning away

leaning back

leaning forward

leg crossing (re-crossing)

nervous tic

rapid breathing

shoulder shrugging

toe tapping

Paralanguage

frogging or croaking voice

long pauses

loud volume/screaming

no pauses

soft volume/whisper

voice breaks

voice slows down

Eye Movement

avoiding eye contact

directional shifts

eye rolling

locked eye contact

rapid blinking

severe gazes

squinting

winks/blinks*

*A wink is not a blink because the wink has intentionality, while the blink tends to be unintentional or involuntary.

There's nothing exhaustive about this list of the most common signals people give off. If you observe a new signal that interests you, just tack it on. The mere act of listing your observations helps cement them in your mind, so that your newly acquired prowess at reading the nonverbal world kicks in more and more automatically from week to week as you strengthen your mental muscles and add new mental skills to your repertoire.

Remember, as part of a complex language, none of these mean anything by themselves; it is only in relationship with each other that we can begin to translate. It is your awareness of them that is paramount.

EYES ON THE WORLD

While I have doubts about the full gamut of what neurolinguistic programming—the notion that we experience the world in one of three ways: visual, auditory, or kinesthetic—can accomplish, it might still be an effective tool to interpret someone's thought processes and analyze their motives. Eyes are especially indicative of what someone is thinking, but it is the direction in which they move that tells us whether someone is thinking in terms of pictures, sounds, or feelings. For example:

- If we visualize something from past experience, our eyes tend to move up and to our left.

- If we are trying to construct a picture from words (to imagine something), our eyes move up and to our right. If we are remembering sounds, our eyes move across to our left, although if we are reconstructing sounds, they move to our right.

- If we are trying to access feelings, our eyes move to the right and down.

- If we are talking to ourselves, our eyes move to the left and down.

- If we de-focus and stare straight ahead, we are thought to be visualizing; that is, thinking more deeply about the picture in our head.

Someone once called the eyes the window of the soul. There's a lot of truth in that expression. The eyes, perhaps more than any other part of us, reflect our attitudes and emotions. They can even betray us, a fact that you can use to your advantage.

To experience how that can work for you, find a willing partner to participate in the following exercise. Ask your partner to place a coin in one hand, then put his hands behind his back and move the coin from hand to hand so that you do not know in which hand the coin ends up. Your partner should then place his closed hands out in front of him. It is now your job to find out where the coin is. If you merely guessed, statistically you'd get it right half the time. But we can do better than that.

Watch your partner's eyes. People usually tend to look away from the hand with the coin, or to unconsciously look directly at it. While these opposite tendencies render the eyes a less than reliable indicator, the nose, no matter which way the eyes are looking, will most likely be pointing to the coin. Keep your eye on the nose, and you'll guess the correct hand more often than not. Subconsciously your partner still wants to look at the coin but doesn't want to use his eyes. So he subtly directs his face to the coin. The best way you, as the observer, can detect this slight movement is by watching his nose. Because your partner has no idea that he is unconsciously giving away the truth, your prowess will leave him dazed and confused.

Eyes can be used to control, too. Just imagine a drill sergeant staring down a recruit. While total eye contact is also indicative of care and love, I can use eye contact to convince my dog that I am the alpha dog in the household, and he has to be submissive to me.

The eyes help us immensely in interacting with other people, as well as with our house pets. Through eye contact we respond to, give feedback, and help regulate the interaction. It's no coincidence that the babies of so many species have large eyes and correspondingly large pupils. We're biologically wired to find those large, dark pupils attractive so that we won't leave our wailing progeny on a mountainside to starve. Similarly, women used to put belladonna drops in their eyes to dilate their pupils, trying to make themselves more attractive to the people around them. Having been a director of research at *Sesame Street*, I know that Jim Henson was acutely aware of this in the designing of the Muppets, which all have exaggerated pupils (as do those widely popular Keane paintings). A dilated pupil has been programmed into our biology to mean the person is in some mode of excitation. We will see in the next chapter how to use this in various propositions.

Just as pupils convey meaning (though most often involuntary), eye contact signals a willingness or unwillingness to interact with someone. Have you ever tried to avoid eye contact with someone because you didn't want to talk to that person? Without eye contact, there is no invitation to interaction. Through eye contact with another person, we develop a kind of bond that enhances the overall process of communication, a nuance most find missing in e-mail and other digitalized forms of communication.

How long we hold eye contact also affects our interaction with others. A glance, which indicates mild or negligible interest, is socially acceptable; a stare, which amounts to an invasion of another's privacy, is not. The only difference is the length of time we're allowed to look. Incidentally, it's speculated that one sure way to let a person know that you're interested in him or her is to hold eye contact a second or two longer than normal, but not long enough to become a stare. Do this several times, and the message should get across. The other person will come across the room and talk to you or run in the opposite direction. Either way, you know your message reached its intended target.

You can create your own catalog of eye movements and eye styles. What kind of attitudes does each of the following indicate to you?

- A blank stare

- A wink

- A glare

- A downcast look

- "Laughing eyes"

- "If looks could kill"

- "She looked daggers at him"

- "Bedroom eyes"

Once you can categorize all of these, you will recognize them again when you see them and easily be able to match the eye expression to the corresponding feeling it invokes. This in turn represents another tool in your nonverbal clue-reading kit. But let's move past the eyes to the rest of our physical beings.

LET'S GET PHYSICAL

Have you ever wondered why grandmothers portrayed in the movies or on television are often rarely tall and skinny, or why the leading man is never short and bald? The answer lies in the fact that, no matter what we say, physical characteristics affect the way we respond to others. We tend to make assumptions about people on the basis of the size and shape of their bodies. Research has found that fat body types are seen as warm-hearted and sympathetic, talkative, jovial, and old-fashioned. Muscular body types are judged as self-reliant, strong, and adventurous, while thin body types are seen as quiet, pessimistic, and suspicious. Oddly enough, while stereotyping can be dangerous, there is some validity in these basic assumptions. Looking at me—a short, stocky, bald Jewish guy—you would assume that I would be warm-hearted, sympathetic, jovial, and talkative. And you would be right. My wife and kids will attest to all that, especially the last point. But that doesn't sum me up, any more than any stereotype sums up anyone.

Other physical characteristics that impact meaning include such things as the length, color, and style of one's hair; the color and condition of one's skin; body odors; and physical defects. When I traveled to Europe for my first performance overseas, I was told that I should cut off my ponytail or people would think I was an aging hipster. I resisted. I liked my ponytail, it was the only hair I had. But I cut it off because I did not want to send a negative message. It ended up being the right choice.

Even locations have physical characteristics that can be read by the trained mind. When I'm traveling, I'm often in the situation of looking for a decent restaurant, so I use my training to locate my best shot at really excellent cooking. The obvious stuff comes first: cleanliness, busy-ness, and a general air of prosperity. Then I study the more subtle clues: Are the people at the tables locals? Is the staff smiling? Is the ethnicity of the place represented by its clientele (Chinese people in a Chinese restaurant, Indians in an Indian restaurant, etc.)? I've had many an excellent meal at some pretty out-of-the-way places, all because I could read the signs. And now so can you.

YOU ARE WHAT YOU WEAR

Clothes don't make the man (or the woman), but they, along with your facial expression and your body language, sure can be revealing. What you wear—including your clothes, your jewelry, and your accessories—are all message-carriers that act as nonverbal stimuli. Even the scent of the soap you use and the perfume you prefer make up part of the package of cues you present to the world.

The first impression that we get is usually not the physical stature or the body language. First, we are looking at what we see, which basically is what people are wearing. Not until then do you begin to study the person and begin to see what they're doing with their hands or the tone of voice they use. That could, indeed, as I say, trump the clothing. But the clothes do make the man or the woman, at least in terms of first impression. While it sounds like a cliché that you don't get a second chance to make a first impression, we do encode our thoughts about people based on what we first feel about them, and we have to work all that much harder to change those impressions.

In my undergraduate years, I had long hair and dressed in jeans—de rigueur for a college student then. At a department store, I opened a door for a woman who was entering. "I'm surprised that a person like you has such manners," she said. One can argue that she shouldn't have made such a snap judgment about me. But that's what we do. What we wear, how we look, even how we smell provide a shorthand for others to make meaning out of us.

While clothes convey meaning, context is the most important thing. A man wearing an old cheap outfit and an expensive watch could indicate that he stole the watch, that it's an heirloom, or that he's more comfortable dressing casually. The circumstances in which you see him and the array of nonverbal clues you pick up will help explain what seems to be an inconsistency. See the world with open and analytical eyes.

That said, I think that everybody, whether they think so or not, dresses with intentionality, and if there's no intentionality, that's intentional, too. Pulling out the first thing in your closet says that you don't care how you look. As I've pointed out before, we cannot *not* communicate. Your artifact language—jewelry, rings, watches—also conveys meaning. For most, a little bling goes a long way.

By knowing what these togs and accessories are saying, you can put your best foot forward and know what others are unwittingly saying about themselves. Some messages are deliberate attempts to position the wearer as the top dog. That's what so-called power suits and power ties are all about. For years, the color to opt for if you wanted to get noticed was red. Then everybody started to wear red, so the color changed. This year the power color seems to be purple or bright lavender or even pink. Those who want to fade into the background opt for more muted colors or for earth tones.

Colors, in the western world, can convey meaning, whether we want them to or not.

See how you intuitively interpret color . . . match up the colors with what you think they provide our senses if one were to wear a tie or sit in a room of that hue.

1. Red	A. Intensity, anxious, mystery, power (7)
2. Blue	B. Heat, excitement, happiness, blood (1)
3. Yellow	C. Coolness, leisure, dignity, truth (2)
4. Orange	D. Joy, light, cold purity, innocence (9)
5. Purple	E. Joyfulness, cheerful glamour, brightness (3)
6. Green	F. Stateliness, dignified wisdom, victory (5)
7. Black	G. Melancholia, neutral, protection, atonement (8)
8. Brown	H. Stimulation, defiant, annoying (4)
9. White	I. Harmony, freshness, stability (6)

Your choice of color impacts others' perception—and reception—of you, and therefore should be situation-dependent. I counsel lawyers to dress well but not over the top when giving their summations, which means opting for a well-tailored dark suit but skipping the red or purple tie. A lawyer doesn't want to antagonize the jury by looking loud, but he or she does want to look fit. Indeed, he or she will want to dress more sharply than the jury, because they are trying to lead its members to a specific conclusion, and people follow those whom they perceive to be of slightly higher status.

In short, if you want to exude control, dress better than the person or people with whom you're meeting. By contrast, at the office dressing for success means dressing the way your immediate supervisor does (or one person above that if you wish to be seen as competitive). Because so much about our clothing sets up our identity and our expectations of others, this is a nonverbal way of helping your supervisor feel that you are just like him or her. It shows that you understand the image you want to project: one of competence and a willingness to integrate yourself into the work environment.

Choosing *not* to wear the office uniform, while potentially risky, is a way of saying to your more formally dressed colleagues that you are a free spirit, an iconoclast, and above petty office policies. (Either that or you didn't get the memo.) And all without saying a word.

Of course, how we accent our words when we do choose to use them also reveals a lot.

YOU TALKIN' TO ME?

How often have you heard the remark, "It's not what you say, it's how you say it"? Paralanguage deals with the *how* and not the *what* of spoken language. It encompasses the vocal elements of rate (how fast), pitch (how high or low), volume (how loud), timbre (tone quality such as harsh, scratchy, soft, etc.), articulation (how precisely the sounds are made), and rhythm (how pauses are used). Without this skill, you're only getting a fraction of the total message. As we established earlier, awareness is knowledge. Knowledge is power.

As with physical characteristics, we tend to stereotype people on the basis of their voices. Recall a time when you "met" someone by phone. As you talked, you probably began to build a mental picture of that person on the basis of his or her voice. Someone once told me that I "look just like I sound." That person had visualized me on the basis of my voice and, in his estimation, had gotten a pretty accurate picture of me.

What personal characteristics are conveyed by the voice? Often we can tell sex, approximate age, race, social status, level of education, and geographical home just from vocal cues. The voice is also an indicator of emotion; recall the voice of someone trying to talk through tears of grief, or the voice of someone full of joy and excitement. This is perhaps one of the most important dimensions of nonverbal communication.

More often than not people don't realize what their tone reveals about how they really feel about what they're saying. Yet tone conveys an unbelievable amount of information. When I call my wife when I'm out on the road (and unfortunately I'm away a lot), I can tell as soon as she answers the phone how she's feeling. It all registers in the tenor of her voice—which lacks life and resonance, sounding flat as a result—and the fact that I know her very well. Hesitation is another indicator that something is up, even if that something is that the caller simply wants to be with you and has nothing much to say.

Too many of us, however, don't listen well, or listen at all. That's about to change, starting with you. Try this: Next time you're on the phone with a friend, see if you can listen to the sound of the words she's using and determine how she's feeling. It takes a little practice, but if you pay attention to the nuances of her speech, you will pick up on sad tones, suppressed elation, and even hidden anger. Imagine how surprised she'll be when you say, "Gosh, when were you going to tell me about the wonderful thing that has happened since we last talked?" or "I'm getting a sense that you're angry with me. What have I done?" That sensitivity will not only endear you to the people around you, but it will also give you one more way to dial in to the thoughts and feelings of others.

Gradually the observational abilities that you've developed will pay off. In a week you will be considerably more observant than you are today. After 2 weeks you'll be alert to nuances that seem elusive now. In a month, with little effort, you'll be an observational wizard. You will be able to pick up each of the mannerisms sent almost constantly, both by friends and strangers. That will allow you to interpret not only what they're thinking but how they're feeling as well. Talk about having a leg up!

TRY THIS

The world of gestures and body positioning is no longer a mystery. You can read the faces, movements, hesitations, and tics of both your friends and of total strangers. Your sensitivity to and receptivity of nonverbal cues have never been better tuned. Right? Let's check.

Engage Your Imagination

Get together with one or two friends and ask that they bring along a few photographs of adults you don't know. Consider the first photograph carefully and make the following determinations:

Is the person married?
Does the person have children?
What does this person do for a living?

Is the person an introvert or an extrovert?

What's this person's favorite hobby or pastime?

This is one of my favorite games. I am always amazed at the revelations of novices. You may not be 100 percent accurate at all times, but you will be accurate most of the time. Don't try to make it happen, but just go with the flow. Make believe you actually know the person. *Let* it happen.

Does practice make perfect? Chart how many times you came up with correct answers to find out.

	Photo #1	Photo #2	Photo #3	Photo #4	Photo #5	Photo #6	Photo #7	Photo #8
Marital Status								
Children								
Occupation								
Personality								
Pastime								

Finally, as awareness builds power and perceptive abilities, scan the world of news and culture for ways that language and nonverbals are having their impact on you daily.

As I write this:

A debate rages on the Photoshop manipulation of CBS TV anchor-to-be Katie Couric. Apparently a press photo promoting her as the first of her gender to host an evening news show has her 20 pounds lighter. This digital diet says reams about the triumph of form over function when it comes to women in our culture.

(continued on page 62)

7 TOOLS OF VERBAL POWER

While negative self-talk and poor communication to others can destroy a relationship, certain verbal ploys can aid, guide, and manipulate your boss, coworkers, or paramour.

1. First it is important to keep in mind that all information is processed through *their* criteria. You can use this fact *to discover and use another's criteria, to obtain their enthusiastic agreement.* That person's criteria magically and irresistibly influence them.

To determine another's criteria ask these questions:

- What makes this important to them?
- What does this do for them?
- What would I have to do to…?
- What would have to happen for…(you to support me?)

Having determined the other's magic words, use these exact words exactly as *they* have used them to create a powerful influence. If they mispronounce or misuse words, then you should mispronounce and misuse them, too. Just as they did. When you do this, you can frame your message in a way that is magically irresistible to the listener!

2. Use the word "you" often. Make the other person feel important and clearly the focus of your intentions. "I enjoy being with you." "I like working with you." "What do you like to do in your spare time?" "What do you think of grouse hunting?"

I think you get the idea.

3. Admiration/flattery work almost every time. But be subtle. Compliment a tie, a fragrance, knickknack…but don't be overly effusive.

4. Learn the secret of hidden emphasis *to influence unknowingly!*

By emphasizing certain words in your sentences, you can give hypnotic commands to others to do what you want. To use this technique you have to plan it. Say you want another to agree with your proposal and sign the agreement.

"Let's summarize, I don't know whether **you agree with this proposal, you** would want to **decide** before **you sign here!** Right on the line." (Strengthen your voice and look the person in the eyes when you say the words in bold.) If you have spoken the words in bold in a different way from usual, then the listener's unconscious mind will hear: "you agree with this proposal…you…decide…you sign here." At one level the listener hears the whole speech, but the words said differently are noticed unconsciously and grouped together. Because they are embedded, the commands do not create so much resistance as simply saying them would.

A more subtle example is: "This a bad **sign,** I can't find my pen. Oh **this** isn't it. Ah, this will do, or at least be acceptable for **now!**"

You emphasize or mark certain words in the sentence in various ways:

Say these words loudly or more softly

Look the other person in the eye as you say these words

Nod your head as you say these words

Make a sign with your hand as you say these words

Open your eyes wider or close them sleepily as you say these words

5. Use the voice of authority.

Drop the tone on the end of a sentence and people know you mean business. Our parents did it when we were young, our teachers did it when we were older, our bosses do it now. After years of learning this, none of us can avoid being affected by it. This voice sounds firm and in our own best interest. Begin to listen to the sound of people's voices. Do they have a childish whining voice? Or the voice of authority?

(continued on next page)

7 TOOLS OF VERBAL POWER (CONTINUED)

When we hesitate because we feel unsure, say when asking a question, our voice tone rises. We become more screechy! When we make a statement, our voice tone drops. A skillful speaker can use intonation to completely change the meaning of the words! We respond more to intonation patterns than to meaning! We do this unconsciously anyway. Learn to hear the patterns and use them consciously.

TV and radio anchors receive training on how to speak using the authority voice, because *how* they say things has greater impact than *what* they say. The same thing can be said in one voice—a voice of authority—and we believe it. Said in another voice, we might not believe it.

We need to practice this because when under stress our voice tone tends to rise, making us sound childish and weak.

When you use the voice of authority, you will automatically become more powerful and influential.

6. Say less than necessary. When you are trying to influence people with words, the more you say, the more common you appear, and the less in control. Even if you say something trivial, it will seem original if you make it vague and enigmatic. Powerful people impress and intimidate by saying less. The more you say, the more chance you have of losing control and/or looking stupid.

7. The most important weapon in your verbal arsenal is to call the other person by name. To know and use her name often creates an almost magical state of control and attention.

Airports are overrun with delays as we go through each individual's belongings, rather than using the shorthand of profiling and looking at physical manifestations of state-of-mind that have succeeded in keeping Israeli airports safe for decades. PC is not necessarily the best way to get things done.

JonBenet Ramsey is in the news again as a man claims he is the murderer. The press frenzy blinded too many to the fact that there is nothing there. On the day after the arrest, I appeared on Court TV's Catherine Crier show to make it clear that the man's affect, the way he basked in the flashing of bulbs, his internal inconsistencies led me to conclude that he was not the one.

> I do not want you to be left with the impression that the verbal world holds no impact. It is the other, if somewhat noisier, strand of the communication DNA.

Dr. Henry Lee, who appeared with me, agreed that the forensic work and previous lie detection reads were also faulty. WE CANNOT BELIEVE OUR EYES AND EARS.

An older athlete usually, we believe, would lose against a much younger opponent. Yet this past week Andre Agassi, at 36, won his U.S. Open tennis matches against 21-year-old Marcos Baghdatis . . . after a grueling 3-hour-and-48-minute match. Prepare to be surprised and look beneath the surface.

MIND BUILDER

Your ability to send and receive nonverbal communication depends a lot on your sensitivity to your environment. You can increase that by taking a shower, eating a meal, or going on a guided walk with your eyes closed.

I do not want you to be left with the impression that the verbal world holds no impact. It is the other, if somewhat noisier, strand of the communication DNA.

CHAPTER 4

STILL MAKING MEANING

SECRETS AND LIES

Now that you have your observational abilities tuned to verbal and nonverbal cues, it's time to learn a little more about the ways these subtle clues can be used and abused by those who might want to deceive us. Face it—at some time or another, everyone lies. So you need to learn how to read those signs as well in order to detect fact from fiction and rarely, if ever, be successfully lied to again.

Because the body usually echoes what the mind is thinking, nonverbal and verbal cues most often work together to reinforce and confirm one another. In fact, should they seem to conflict, consider that a red flag: The speaker's intent is at odds with his words. When someone bangs the table and yells, odds are they are faking being angry. If they yell and then bang the table, the emotion is more genuine, since the natural progression is first the vocalization of a feeling and then the physical response. A man on a date may talk a good line in order to project a feeling of self-confidence, but his date (who has read this book and actively participated in the program) can detect his insecurity through the fact that he keeps his hands in his pockets the whole night.

Once you know what to look for, a person's body being out of sync with his words can be as obvious as a bad actor on a stage. It's up to you to read the mismatched cues and gestures of others carefully to determine the reason and gain the upper hand in a negotiation. If your boss says something complimentary and then points at you in a way that could easily seem accusatory, he may be hiding something from you. Changes in his or her tone of voice when talking to you may signal an untruth, or at the very least indicate a subject of personal discomfort. Similarly, sudden over-friendliness and sudden coldness, in spite of any words involved, should make you pay extra attention.

Though these body cues are invaluable, it is still fair to say that the face usually gives away a liar. The face is our emotional register, especially where deceit is concerned. Liars have also been known to smile more and talk less (they may even fumble for their words when they speak). This is just another case of the body's resistance to lying and the kinds of cues you can pick up as to someone's truthfulness or guilt. Someone being underhanded may also wish to cover her mouth, as though she could cover the lie as she says it. The hand that normally covers the mouth is the left hand, irrespective of whether the person concerned is right- or left-handed. Why? I don't know, perhaps it is the subordinate hand, but it's true, and it's something you can watch for, especially when children are involved since they often cover their mouths when telling whoppers.

Liars can try to hide, but their innermost deceptions are, to me and now to you, as plain as the nose on their face. You just have to know what to look for.

THE FAMOUS AND THE INFAMOUS

Given my line of work, I am often asked about the guilt or inno-cence of people in the news. When I guested for an hour on the Maury show I was shown video news clips and asked for my evalu-ations (similar to what I now do on a regular basis for Court TV). I have to tell you up front that I don't "do" guilt and innocence. I'm not a judge, and I don't want to get in trouble with potentially dangerous people or put someone under a shadow of suspicion just on my say-so. I simply look for cues that belie discomfort and point to untruths.

In brief:

O.J. was asked if he had anything to do with the murders of his ex-wife and her friend. His response was, "I'm 100 percent innocent." As he said this, his eyes blinked in the longest, slowest blink I have ever witnessed. This is not necessarily to say that he is guilty of murder, only that that statement was probably a lie. Children often close their eyes when telling untruths, thinking on some level that if they can't see you, you can't see them (lying). O.J. seemed to be covering the same territory.

Bill Clinton lowered his chin and pulled it in when he discussed "that woman." No other Clinton speech showed the normally "chin up" effusive former president take such an evasive nonverbal position. Conversely, when I was asked by *McCall's* to review Hillary Clinton's appearance on the *Today* show, I asserted  that she honestly believed her husband's proclamation of innocence. Her steady gaze and genuine smile convinced me of that.

In the televised portion of the talks about the Iraq war, Colin Powell spoke easily, extemporaneously, and with a full belief in what he was saying. In contrast, the ambassador from Spain kept her hand over her mouth as though trying to keep her words from betraying her. The French ambassador broadcast his distaste for the whole proceedings by leaning back, putting his hands to his head, and crossing his arms, as though he could stop any information from reaching him. I said this live on Australian TV; it took several years to find that Powell too was deceived. And President Bush? As always, he came across, *at that time*, as completely sincere. He believed what he said.

Outside the world of politics, people like Winona Ryder and Martha Stewart show themselves to be consummate actresses. They feigned shock at the charges against them—the hesitation between the accusation and the protestation is measurable—and seemed to be most concerned with how to protect their public persona and get the best spin from the experience of being accused.

Scott Peterson, accused of murdering his wife and unborn baby, showed no affect whatsoever, but even this total shutdown of external emotions was a signal. He was trying his best to give nothing away, and in doing so he gave away the fact that he had something to hide. Compare this to Mark Karr, who gave away a full admission, basked in its glory, and was innocent (though he did believe at times that it was true). The pathological mind is the hardest to read . . . if they believe, you get the right cues, but you can be wrong.

Of course, you don't have to be famous (or infamous) to lie.

THE WHOLE TRUTH

People lie all the time to help protect themselves. So it helps if you know what to look for when trying to ascertain someone's truthfulness. The job interview offers a classic—and well-trodden—

arena for deception. Indeed, in a survey of 1,500 companies it was found that 71 percent had encountered serious lying on resumes. The most common lies on resumes were 31 percent about previous experience, 21 percent about university qualifications, 19 percent about salary, and 18 percent about secondary qualifications (see "Lies, Damn Lies and Résumés" by Kate Thomas, *Forbes*, June 2006).

So how does the interviewer—or a police interrogator, for that matter—manage the situation? One suggestion involves using subtle rewards and punishments when distinguishing between perceived truths and lies. For example, if the interviewee appears to be speaking honestly, then:

- The response from the person conducting the interview should be friendly and open, e.g., the "palms-up" gesture
- First names should be used
- The interrogator should look directly at and smile at the interrogated
- Personal space can be increased between the two of them by leaning or moving back

On the other hand, if the interrogated appears to be departing from the truth, then the response can be more confrontational. For example, the interrogator can:

- Use gestures such as finger pointing
- Gaze at the individual for slightly longer than usual or look away
- Use the subject's surname rather than first name, or even
- Lean forward to decrease personal space

The aim here is to counter the apparent deception and draw it out into the open.

ALL STRESSED UP AND NO PLACE TO GO

Stress can be a sign of deception. This is manifested in mannered behavior that seems out of place, or uncharacteristic of the individual. As early as 1905 Sigmund Freud wrote, "He that has eyes to see and ears to hear may convince himself that no mortal can keep a secret. If his lips are silent, he chatters with his fingertips. Betrayal oozes out of every pore."

Stress can indicate deception through:

- Making odd facial expressions
- Feigning yawns
- Rubbing hands together
- Picking fingernails
- Stretching
- Avoiding eye contact
- Pausing for longer than usual, or going silent
- Exhibiting glazed expressions
- Repeatedly clearing the throat
- Making speech errors
- Alternating the pitch of the voice
- Grinding teeth, biting lips, nose touching
- Twirling hair

Keep in mind that our internal discomfort with the act of lying produces these self-betrayals. And they're completely unconscious—we don't and can't control them. They're out there for anyone with the ability to read them, as long as you're dealing with someone who is not a psychopath. If someone doesn't feel guilty about lying, no signals are given off.

Similarly, if someone believes what he's saying, even if it's not true, you will not be able to detect the deception. Eli Wallach at the Actors Studio, for example, asked me if the late Marlon Brando would have been able to successfully lie to me. I answered in the affirmative. Consumed by whatever role he decided to play, Brando, a great Method actor, would actually become that character and thus would not in actuality have been lying, since he believed implicitly what he was saying. Or as George Costanza said, "It's not a lie if you believe it's true." Self-deception is a powerful defender of our delicate psyches.

In some cases, individuals under suspicion decrease their normal expressive hand and arm movements, using them instead to soothe the nose, mouth, and brow. "Picking lint" can also be seen as characteristic of guilty behavior. Of course, all of these behaviors could be just that particular individual's way of getting through the day and indicative of nothing more than the fact that their nose itches and they happen to be wearing a linty sweater. A baseline is usually called for.

It is that all-important baseline of behavior that you have to be familiar with before you can tell whether the fidgeting is a normal part of their life or whether it is a deviation from the norm and therefore a clue that they are uncomfortable with what they are saying. Though as you shall see, there are some quick reads that raise red flags in many situations

So let's get down to the nitty-gritty of lie detection.

TO TELL THE TRUTH

I once suspected a student of plagiarism but was unable to find the original source. As I talked to the student about something else in the paper, I suddenly asked, "Did you copy this?"

The student glanced down briefly, then looked up and said, "No." This gave me enough to know that I must dig deeper.

Let me explain why.

It's not always important for someone to look you straight in the eye. Good liars can gaze at you unblinking for hours. I can look you straight in the eye and say, "I have a full head of hair." Check the cover. This is—and you must excuse me here—a bald-faced lie. Looking someone in the eye is not in itself an indicator of much of anything, but it becomes important when the direct stare is a deviation from the person's normal eye patterns. Conversely, if a person looks you in the eye until you ask a direct question and then glances off, that may be your cue.

My success in using cues to determine the truthfulness of statements has garnered me considerable attention and work for corporations, the judicial system, police, and security agencies. All this experience has further honed my lie-detecting abilities: Even for me, practice never quite makes perfect, but it sure gets me close.

If all these professional liars can't pull a fast one on me, needless to say I rarely have a problem spotting liars in my day-to-day life or during my performances. One thing I like to do in my stage show is call five people up onstage and ask them to draw a simple picture. I select a drawing at random and ask each person if they drew it. They have been instructed to say "no," so that one person, the one who actually drew the picture, is lying. I show them each the picture and ask each, "Did you draw this?" With amazing regularity, my subjects display a tight range of cues that allow me to spot the liar every time. Remember, telling an untruth is an uncomfortable act for anyone but a pathological liar, so that discomfort shows up and you have to be ready to read it.

One person will try to stare right through me, as though eye contact were a way to establish innocence. That's his picture.

One person will glance at how the other people are answering. This unconscious reaction is another way we display discomfort with a lie: We see if anyone has caught us out. That's her picture.

Another person will look me in the eye until they answer my question. Then he looks away. That's his picture.

The next person will move her head back and forth with just too much vigor while she is saying no. Her body, again, is trying to tell the truth, even though she's been instructed to lie. That's her picture.

The fifth picture, well, since there's only one person left, you can figure that out.

Any or all of these cues, including any slight verbal stutters and hesitations, can be picked up by any of us, and all, working together in context, can indicate a lie.

I don't always identify each and every onstage liar, but I have a pretty good track record. Spotting the telltale signs of deceit, however, can be tricky, especially since some people can be devilishly good at lying. Unfortunately for the aspiring Lie Detector, mistakes will be made. Still, these basic clues go a long way toward successfully detecting lies. At the very least they raise red flags that indicate that deeper exploration is required.

Children persistently try to deceive their parents, so much so that the parent becomes adept at spotting little Johnny "trying to pull the wool over their eyes" by his facial expression, his speech pattern, his hand movements, and his inability to look at his parent. But with kids, the parent also becomes an expert in how to handle the kinds of lies they tell, and learns through experience which lies need to be dealt with and which lies are better ignored. After all, you must choose your battles. If my son lied about borrowing the car without permission, or drinking milk from the carton, I cannot give both equal weights as a lie.

We've already seen how facial expressions can contradict a person's words, thereby revealing a lie. Similarly, someone who is being deceitful and lying may move their feet, torso, and legs around a lot, or remain stiffly still. This is a sign of feeling uncomfortable, and pointing a toe or limb toward the nearest exit will underline the fact that the person concerned wishes to get the conversation over with and leave. He may well rub the side of his nose or his eyes, hold the back of his neck, or clutch his throat, lick his lips, or even sweat profusely, all because he feels uncomfortable with his deceit. As such, he will try to keep a distance between himself and his audience, so as to maintain a barrier of safety.

Other cues? It is well known that when people tell lies or even hear other people lying, they often tend to touch their nose. There seems to be two explanations for this gesture. Firstly, by touching the nose the hand also covers the mouth where the lies are coming from. Secondly, when people tell lies, it causes stress, and stress causes the skin to get slightly hotter. When the skin gets hotter, the nose, which is a sensitive organ, may itch or expand slightly so the individual touches the itching nose.

In the case of someone trying to be open, there may often be an open-handed signal—this shows honesty. Usually, when people are being honest, their hands are readily visible. On the other hand, the dishonest among us may feel slightly guilty and try to hide our hands by putting them behind our back, in our pockets, or folding our arms. However, it is worthwhile considering that someone who is trying to deceive may seek to do so by actually showing his hands, palms upward, and shrugging, as if to say that he can't help himself, thereby enlisting our sympathy for his or her case. See? It's tricky! You must look at all the signals together because they work as a package. It's never one clue in isolation from the rest, but always that clue in relationship to the rest of the verbal or nonverbal language. A smile when punched in the stomach usually does not indicate happiness.

This stuff isn't black and white. You have to take in a lot of information and sift through it. For instance, people who are being deceitful may find it difficult to maintain eye contact. They will not look at us when we are talking, nor when they are talking, and may often be looking downward. Conversely they may stare directly into our eyes with no lateral movement at all. Clearly identify the signs, and don't assume that because people look away all the time and seem nervous and/or preoccupied that they are being deceitful.

LISTEN UP

As helpful as visible clues can be when ascertaining whether someone is telling the truth, they pale next to auditory clues. Pay close attention and you can almost always hear a lie. But you must train yourself to listen, not just to hear.

In order to hear distortions and variances of speech, one of the most reliable ways to discern the subtext of what's being said or to disarm a lie, you have to know how to really listen. Often, we're so busy trying to figure out how we're going to respond during a conversation that we barely hear or absorb the words, let alone the nuances. So stop planning your next brilliant quip and listen for not only the words but also the ways in which they are said. The following mindscript will help you practice your listening skills.

NOW HEAR THIS MINDSCRIPT

This mindscript will enhance your listening skills and abilities.

Close your eyes and allow yourself to enter the total relaxed state.

Visualize your ears as a powerful antenna, absorbing and processing even the quietest sounds around you.

See your ears as powerful vacuuming devices focusing in on sounds that are meaningful.

Tell yourself that your powers of listening and hearing will be sharper and clearer. Picture your aural powers being sharper and clearer.

Notice that your mind tingles in anticipation of the new way that you will hear.

Reinforce this feeling of relaxation using imagery and suggestions of your own choosing before bringing this exercise to an end.

ESTABLISH BASELINES—LISTEN WITH ALL YOUR SENSES

Brief distortions serve as signals. Momentary changes are what you should concentrate on here—the nuances in the person's speech that can indicate discomfort with what they're saying. Again, you have to establish a baseline for this person so you can tell when he or she deviates from it, but with more practice in really listening you can learn to do that more quickly. So listen up!

How often do you listen in an average day? Certainly more than you speak, but much less than you think you do. Listening doesn't involve merely hearing. It is an active approach, an attitude, a way in which you relate to the world. To be good at it you must make it a part of the way you live. You have to be able to listen, and listen well, to perceive the subtle differences between lies and truth.

That isn't easy. Focused listening, like observation, takes a bit of practice. Take in whole conversations and then try to summarize what you hear and how it is being said. Pay attention to how words are being used, what is being emphasized, and what the sound of the entire exchange is like.

It is not only the tone or the sound itself that matters but also the context. Tone becomes important only when it's inconsistent—discordant, jarring to the ears. An automobile engine rattles before gaining power; a computer grinds upon start-up. A baby cries for a brief moment in the night. A stairway creaks in an empty house. These sounds are inconsistent and therefore get your attention. You can hear the same sorts of inconsistencies in speech. And that's your cue to listen more closely. These can be alerts that the speaker is uncomfortable with what is being said, and therefore may be lying.

Vocal tones vary from person to person, but each individual usually speaks with a steady tone. What becomes significant is the moment when the steadiness varies, creating a tonal distortion, if only for a split second. Prolonged distortions are easy to hear, like screaming, sobbing, high-pitched hysteria—and their reason is usually obvious. Distortions that betray lies are subtler. Here's what to listen for:

- A rise or fall in pitch or register, especially if it is quickly corrected. When a voice changes from low to high and then back to low, something is probably wrong with what is being said.

- Changing rate or rhythm of speaking, as when someone interjects a brief staccato burst of words into an otherwise steady monologue, or changes his or her usual conversational rhythm and sustains the change. If a gruff person becomes gentle, or a bubbly type becomes withdrawn, it's a signal that calls for decoding. Indeed, any change in rate or rhythm is worth pondering.

- Force, the strength applied to a single word or phrase. Force can convey more meaning than the speaker intends because emphasis is usually unconscious.

- Cracking voice, when there is no physiological reason for it (so discount this with teens), and other vocal incongruities. People's voices tend to change because they are afraid, excited, or aroused in some manner, either pleasurably or not.

Telling a lie can be one cause for vocal variation, but not the only one, as the following scenario will demonstrate:

Me: What time will you be home?
Teenage son: Around 10:30.

> Me: Where are you going?
> Teenage son: (with a groan) I'm not sure yet.

That purely instinctive groan signals deep resistance to the question (though again it does not necessarily indicate a lie). Deeper investigation may be called for.

- If you hear a slight stammer or slurring and if it's uncharacteristic, pay attention.

> Me: Why aren't you coming to my party?
> Colleague: 'Cause I-I-I've got a lot of work to do . . . I, uh,
> it's important . . . the, uh, boss, um, wants it tomorrow.

That kind of response raises additional questions. Why isn't he more coherent? What is he hiding?

I can't emphasize this enough: You have to listen with all your senses. Look and listen for things that are incongruent, where the packet of signals does not seem to work together. The evidence is everywhere. Just look and listen. Even at a social gathering.

Here is a simple example of the method at work. You're a single woman, alone at a party. An attractive man approaches, making conversation. If you're interested, you may be likely to ask, "Are you married?" If he says no, he might be single. Or he might be lying. Unless he is truly pathological, subtle clues will point to the lie.

As I've explained, we all experience a bit of discomfort when lying. While we may say one thing, our nonverbal expression, over which we have little control, says another. This nonverbal, uncontrollable behavior is, in the traditional literature, called leakage. Simply put, leakage is the information that seeps out of us in spite of what our words say, i.e., all of the body and facial language discussed in the previous chapter.

At the party above watch for the nearly imperceptible half nod of the head before he says no. The combination of a no and a half nod translates into a probable yes. The half nod was obviously unconscious—and that tends to be more truthful than the conscious.

If he is looking directly at you when he says no, watch to see if his eyes close or if he looks at the floor. Either can represent a denial of the word no.

Does he raise his drink to his lips, or cough, or rub his nose while saying no? This is a red flag. If he shifts his feet or plays with his tie, he may be very married—or just very nervous. Your perceptions of the total person, the number of inappropriate gestures, and the context of the situation provide you with the tools you need to make the distinction.

If he makes a joke ("No, do I look married?"), you could consider the response witty. But it's a diversion at best—perhaps from lack of confidence. At worst it's an evasion.

With more than three such contradictory signals, you are on solid ground to doubt his veracity.

A real no requires only the word *no*—nothing else.

THE TRUTH DETECTIVES

Those who investigate the honesty of others need to be able to spot the telltale signs of deception without making it obvious that they are doing so. To some extent this relies upon common sense and intuition, although training is needed to develop and improve those skills.

You the reader can use these same techniques or insights when determining veracity. Any or all of the following should be treated as indicative of possible lying:

• Fail to answer the question asked

• Pretend not to understand it

- Remain silent

- Feign emotion, such as anger

- Pretend they are feeling ill

If they can't get away with concealing what they are doing, they may then begin to falsify the situation by:

- Inventing a scenario

- Creating a tall story

- Telling a lie

To conceal or avoid telling direct lies, people often water down their statements. Richard Nixon's famous counter to the allegation that he authorized the Watergate break-in—"The president would not do such a thing"—is a classic example of this. By depersonalizing the act and taking the "I" out of the equation, he absolved himself of responsibility for it. For those whose task it is to elicit the truth from individuals suspected of deception, the type of questions asked and the nature of the answers given are all-important. Questions should be directly aimed: "When did YOU" or "Are YOU sure," etc. Demand exactness and cut through ambiguity.

A word of warning to the overzealous (along with all the rest of you): Nonverbal communication provides clues to how people think and feel, *not* evidence. I cannot emphasize enough how vital it is to make sure that you take into account all the signs being displayed. For example, the open-handed gesture with shoulder shrug on its own is not a sign of deceitfulness, but more a case of being unable to say anything about a situation. Again, however, this raises a red flag and bears closer scrutiny.

It is probably safe to assume that most politicians bear watching as well, especially since their gestures so regularly indicate that they are covering up something. Iranian president Mahmoud Ahmadinejad was unblinking during his *60 Minutes* interview. In addition to chin maneuvers during his nationally aired testimony, President Bill Clinton touched his nose about every couple minutes and performed micro shrugs at crucial moments. When uncomfortable with what he's saying during television interviews, President George W. Bush routinely displays a wide range of nonverbal tics ranging from rapid eye blinks to a curled lip. I suspect that the nonverbal cues displayed by each of these men in these public moments cost them credibility. President Bush's intentional bowlegged macho cowboy swagger borders on simian, but for many Americans it is the regular/tough guy image they love.

There may be up to 1,000 body language cues packed in every minute of interaction—this is how the subconscious mind speaks. No matter how much a person wants to control it, nonverbal behavior reveals how someone truly feels. So here is your viewer's guide of what to look for next time you try to evaluate a politician's veracity. Happy hunting.

- **Sharp pauses.** When a person is lying, they pause longer in the middle of sentences, provide shorter answers to questions, and take longer to begin their response than someone who's merely nervous. After all, they need time to create the lie. However, don't take this cue in isolation. Also check to see where their eyes go after the question. People tend to look up to the right to visualize or invent a response, and down to the right to invent sounds. We often recall the truth by looking up to the left or down to the left.

- **Excessive gesturing.** When people lie, they move their hands a lot and employ "adapters"—that is, nervous movements like scratching the body or fiddling with a pencil. If a candidate is asked a question and immediately picks up a pen and begins playing with it, something's amiss subconsciously. If this juggling seems excessive, and especially if it's combined with other cues, you can bet he's lying. On the other hand . . .

- **Lack of gesturing.** The rehearsed or practiced liar, who has planned his deceit ahead of time, will try to control gestures. Many politicians are coached to stay still during TV appearances. They keep their face inexpressive, upper body stiff, and legs often crossed. Watch then for the leaks when asked surprise questions that demand a deception.

- **Read his lips.** Look for unusual movement of the mouth, lips, or tongue. While discussing weapons of mass destruction in a recent NBC interview, Vice President Cheney pursed his lips and sucked them inward more than half a dozen times. Tight lips indicate you may be planning to keep the truth in. If you actually suck the lips in, you may be withholding anger. A dry cough or cracking voice is a psychological response to the discomfort of lying. When you are nervous, your mouth becomes dry, and you lick your lips and swallow as you struggle to find the right words to say. The Iran Contra hearings saw many who asked for glasses of water.

- **Hand hiding.** Hands symbolically express the emotions of the heart, which is why liars tend to keep them hidden. (Research on handshakes shows that the single most important factor is palm-to-palm contact. When people don't get this contact, they wonder what the other person is hiding.) They'll stick them in their pockets, clench them, or hold them behind their backs. Look to see if the hands are open and in full view. One caveat: People who are nervous tend to hide their hands, too, so look for other cues as well.

- **Creation of barriers.** Just as we pull down the shades when we don't want others to see into our homes, we close off entrances to our body so our true feelings aren't seen. There are windows at the bottom of our feet, kneecaps, bottom of the torso, middle of the chest, neck, mouth, eyes, and top of the head. A liar tends to close off these entrances—putting clothing over them, turning them away from the person he's talking to, putting objects or furniture between himself and others, or simply folding his arms. When someone's windows are closed, we don't feel as comfortable with the interaction. For good reason: They're hiding something.

- **Excessive confidence.** Think of this as the super-smooth salesman effect. He so enthusiastically praises the product that you feel uncomfortable. We look and listen for anything that doesn't sound normal. Nonverbal communication—in this case paralanguage, which includes voice, tone, volume, and speaking rate—that sounds overconfident is read at the subconscious level as out of the norm. Spot a liar by going with your gut impression. If you feel something is out of norm, even if you can't articulate it specifically, you are probably right. Both President Bush and Condi Rice display this behavior.

- **Misalignment of circumstances vs. demeanor.** When former House Representative Tom Delay was discussing his financial shenanigans, one would expect him to be emotionally upset and embarrassed, considering the most powerful man in the U.S. Congress was accused of taking kickbacks. Instead, he remained smiling broadly and was overly calm in press response. This demeanor was not what we expected. The lack of appropriateness was a sign he wasn't being sincere.

- **Half smiles.** A smile is the most common facial expression to mask emotions. It is often used to hide displeasure and anger. As we've already discussed, a real smile changes the entire face. The eyes light up. The forehead wrinkles, the eyebrows and cheek muscles rise, the skin around the eyes and mouth crinkles. And, finally, the mouth turns up. It is slow to occur and slow to disappear. In a masking smile, nothing moves but the corners of the mouth, and often they curve down rather than up. It is quick to appear and vanishes just as speedily.

• Parallel body position and posture. Tony Blair is the master at being Zelig, the Woody Allen creation who becomes similar to anyone he is around. It makes someone comfortable to be with when they mirror you . . . but it does raise questions of what is real and what is merely an act.

Of course, all signals should be taken as a packet that works together. Just because someone appears anxious, for example, does not prove wrongdoing. They could just be nervous. Similarly, the person who blushes, perspires, sweats, trembles, and stutters may also just be nervous and not bent on deceiving his or her audience. To spot a liar or deceiver, listen to what they say, how they say it, whether their speech pattern is different from what is normal for them, whether they are maintaining a distance that again would be abnormal for them, and look for closed and negative gestures. It is the overwhelming preponderance of cues that build up over the course of an interview that can give you enough information to form a solid opinion about the truthfulness of someone's statements.

THE ULTIMATE LIE DETECTION TOOL

Of course some practiced liars—and attentive 6 Keys students—know almost as much about nonverbal communication (or in this case miscommunication) as I do. Case in point:

I had just completed a program for the executives of Chase Manhattan Bank in Palm Springs and was ready to relax. A small group from the conference approached and asked for one more demonstration, this time with a gentleman we will call Barry. Barry was a cynical VP, someone they all felt could easily deceive me.

I asked Barry to sit. "Think of a number from one to 10," I said. I handed him my business card. "Now write down your number and hide it in your hand."

Then I directed him that each time I mentioned a number and asked if he was thinking of it he was to say no, regardless of the number.

He agreed. I stood facing him and slowly counted aloud from one through 10. Something told me this wasn't going to be easy. He was tough, bordering on hostile, and he had the audience—his buddies—on his side.

At two, he looked at me and said NO, *whew*. At three, he folded his arms before replying. At five he blurted out NO. At six he fidgeted in his seat and said N-N-No. If he ever left banking, he could surely make a living as an actor. At seven he bit his lip before responding; he coughed at eight. At 10 he sat rigid before responding. Like I said, he was tough. And he had obviously been listening very carefully when I had explained to his group all of the classic physical cues that can tip off a lie.

"The number you wrote down is three," I concluded, with just a touch of uncertainty.

His triumphant look vanished. He was shocked. He regained his composure and turned over the card. It said three.

"How did you know?" he asked.

"Because you lied at three," I said.

"Yes, but how did you know?" he demanded.

I told him he'd have to buy the book.

Now here it is, for Barry and for you: The answer lay in his eyes, in watching the eyes as he answered *no*. In response to a direct question that causes an internal emotional reaction, the pupils will dilate. You can't fake dilated pupils (well, not unless you've been to the eye doctor that day), and dilated pupils are a sign of excitement

MIND BUILDER

Are you being lied to? With everything you've learned about liars and the ways they give themselves away—from vocal shifts to unintentional body movements to the ways their eyes change—you are well on your way to becoming a walking, talking lie detection machine. How good are you at discerning untruths? Find out by playing a few hands of Liar's Poker.

Find a deck of cards and pull out an equal number of kings and aces. Using this tiny new deck, draw one card at a time and look at it. Do not allow the person you're playing against to see the card. If the card is an ace, you must say so. However, if the card is a king, you can either tell the truth and say that it's a king, or you can lie and say that it's an ace. Your opponent's goal is to try to catch you in the lie.

If you say the card is a king, nothing happens. You can't be lying so no money changes hands. You just take a new card and go again. Indeed, you have to say that a card is a king every now and then because your opponent knows that the deck is one-half kings.

If you say that the card is an ace, your opponent can either Call or Fold.

If she Folds, she loses 50 cents and never finds out whether or not you were bluffing.

and stimulation. Watch your poker buddy or your corporate competitor when he makes a proposal. If his pupils dilate, it could mean he has a great hand. It could also mean he has a lousy hand or a gotcha, but he's definitely excited about something. We've all noticed the wide shining eyes of people coming off a roller coaster, or the big round eyes of the person on the receiving end of a surprise party. There's no way to control that response; it's purely

If she Calls, she gets to see your card and find out if you were bluff-ing or telling the truth. If she Calls and you were bluffing, she wins $1. If she Calls and you were not bluffing, you win $1.

Then switch roles. Use the cues from this chapter to try to read those bluffs.

PERSON 1	Win	Lose
1st Deal		
2nd Deal		
3rd Deal		
4th Deal		
5th Deal		
PERSON 2	Win	Lose
1st Deal		
2nd Deal		
3rd Deal		
4th Deal		
5th Deal		

biological. Beware of the sunglass wearers; unless it's an eye ail-ment, they are hiding something. Ask if they would mind removing it. Be bold. It is your dough on the line.

As we know, anyone who isn't a pathological liar will experi-ence discomfort when telling an untruth, no matter how slight. That discomfort registers in this uncontrollable physical response that gives anyone away, even a tough guy trying to beat me at my own game. In this case, his pupils dilated on the count of three. He couldn't help but betray himself. Neither can almost anyone else. The eyes don't lie.

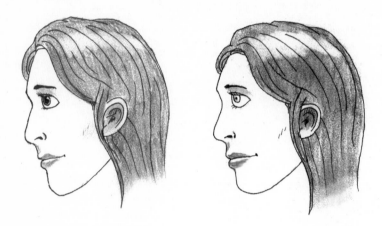

MIND BUILDER

To increase your adeptness at being able to discern when someone is telling the truth or not, watch TV with the sound off, and focus on their expressions and body language instead of their words.

CHAPTER 5

STILL MAKING MEANING — MENTAL MANAGEMENT

ARTS OF POWER AND PERSUASION

For most of us, having successful relationships—whether on the personal or the professional front—is a top priority. You have already discovered that we live in a world of silent messages. To succeed in this nonverbal world where relationships can be made or broken without a word being uttered, you need to make the language of nonverbal communication work for you. By recognizing different gestures, expressions, characteristics, and thought processes, you can not only detect lies but you can also read people— and even yourself—better. And that will help you to relate better in your personal life, and to influence and impress those around you in ways they aren't even aware of.

One young woman I worked with was being overlooked in the office. Intimidated by her supposed superiors, she had subconsciously made choices that rendered her invisible and powerless. Together we reviewed everything from her choice of wardrobe to her body language. And she began to make some changes. She ditched her neutral separates and began to wear colorful suits as her immediate supervisor did. She started looking people in the eye, using a firmer grip when shaking hands, and paralleling body language when in one-on-one meetings. Just as importantly, she began to anticipate what her superiors wanted by learning how to listen to what they weren't saying as readily as what they were saying. Today she is an executive vice president of a Fortune 500 company.

The ability to read people is something we've lost in this modern life. Three hundred years ago, we had to be able to relate to others through direct interactions—to look them in the face and have a conversation. People back then were well versed in reading one another because they did it all the time, and they cared to do it. That skill helped them get along in their world. It wasn't something separate from them, it was integral to their lives.

It still is. You have studied the reading of facial and body language, tone of voice, and you even know how to utilize that information to detect lies. Now it's time to reveal the secrets that can help you control situations and manage relationships. These kinds of body language cues can put you in the winner's seat before you even start. Whether petitioning for a raise at work or negotiating a loan, wooing your main squeeze or denying your children's unreasonable requests, here are the tools to control any situation. You can utilize space and time to win the day. Even the way you talk (or don't talk), dress, or choose to sit can boost your power of persuasion and weaken someone else's position. Not only will this improve your relationships at home, on the job, and elsewhere, but it will improve your bottom line as well. You can profit from your observations about how people position themselves in relation to you— or others they're dealing with face-to-face—by gaining insight into what those tendencies reveal.

SPATIAL BOUNDARIES

Americans, as a rule, need a lot of personal space. We're used to it. America has more space than many other countries, so our personal space is both important to us and more expansive by comparison. We tend to equate space with power. Think about it: The most powerful executive has the largest office; the better one is doing the bigger one's house gets and the more space one has around one's house. When we feel crowded, we move to get our space around us again. I remember a performance where a woman I'd called up from the audience had no sense of my need for personal space. I backed away from her every advance and ended up falling right off the stage!

Spatial boundaries, or "proxemics," have to do with our conceptualization and use of the space around us. Basically, humans are territorial animals. We each stake out some ground and say, "This is mine." Look at all the fences and hedges that lay claim to yards. Each of us has "our" desk in the office, "our" chair in the classroom, "our" corner of a particular room. Think specifically about the desk at which you are sitting and the space around it. Do you sit there every day you come to class or to work? How would you feel if you came into the room and found someone else in "your" chair?

Often our territory is not protected by any physical boundary. Unless we are particularly curious or voyeuristic, we tune out conversations of which we are not a part, and we don't look at couples showing affection in public. While waiting in the doctor's office, we dutifully read our magazines and disregard other patients' conversations with the receptionist. At the very least, we *pretend* to be oblivious to these things. In this way, we demonstrate our respect for the territorial rights of other people.

You have to watch out for others' personal space, too. While walking down a city sidewalk, a friend of mine passed too close to a homeless person's shopping cart and suffered a sharp whack across the shoulders from the furious woman she had impinged on. Apparently, my friend had invaded the woman's space, even though it looked to her like just another stretch of public sidewalk.

Our use and perception of space say a lot about us and are extremely important dimensions of nonverbal communication. Edward T. Hall in his classic *The Silent Language* offers a continuum of personal distance applicable to middle class American culture. At one end is intimate distance, which ranges from actual physical touching to about 18 inches. Casual-personal distance ranges from 18 inches to 4 feet; social-consultive distance ranges from 4 feet to 12 feet; and public distance ranges from 12 feet to the limits of hearing and visibility. Those distances can be relative, so pay attention. You don't want to get it wrong and get whacked for ignoring the cues!

Hall's continuum of personal distance does not apply to other cultures. The notion of personal space is culturally determined. Latin Americans and Middle-Easterners, for example, generally converse much closer to each other than Americans do. In the United States and Western Europe, one's own space is said to be anything under an arm's length; in Mediterranean cultures, it is under elbow length, while in Eastern Europe it is about wrist length. It's easy to see how these different distances can lead to personal—and even global—misunderstandings.

How strongly do you feel about your personal space? When you go into a lecture room, do you choose a seat next to someone, or do you choose a seat that is between two vacant ones? Where do you sit in a movie theater? All I know is, no matter where I sit I'm inevitably right in front of the noisiest person in the theater. All my training, all my picking up of subtle cues, and I can't watch a movie in peace.

TOUCH CONTROL

You can't read just one signal; proximity is just one of a packet of signals that express aspects of a personality. What we do, where we stand, how we look, how we sound, what we wear—all these things, though nonverbal, "say" something. Listen with all your senses. Even touch can communicate hidden thoughts. While touch certainly conveys a wide range of affective emotions, it also controls and guides the behavior of others.

Touching behavior is a basic and extremely important channel of nonverbal communication. It covers a broad range of behaviors from brushing someone in a crowd to a lover's embrace. Touching behaviors tend to personalize communication and are extremely important in emotional situations. Indeed, we react physiologically to touch. Research shows that children who are hugged grow and have greater body-weight growth in early childhood years, and that endorphins fire when we embrace.

How, when, where, and to what extent we touch tells a great deal about us as people and as communicators. Touch in the form of finger pointing, poking, and tapping can be read as an expression of power. Robert Caro writes of President Johnson in his definitive biography *The Years of Lyndon Johnson*:

"He used his stories, and he used his jokes, he used his promises, used his threats, backing senators up against walls or trapping them in their chairs, wrapping an arm around their shoulders and thrusting a finger in their chests, grasping lapels, watching their hands, watching their eyes, listening to what they said, or to what they didn't say: 'The greatest salesman one on one who ever lived'—trying to make his biggest sale."

Knowing that can help you consciously modify your behavior to elicit the reaction you're seeking, and to correctly interpret others' signals.

TOUCH: CULTURAL NORMS/SOCIAL CONTROL

Touching in our society is controlled by strong social norms. A baby's first touch is the warmth and security of a blanket in its mother's arms. As it grows, it is comforted and caressed by parents and generally feels no shame in that warm experience. This is fine, until the child reaches puberty and the unwritten social commandment THOU SHALT NOT TOUCH is abruptly handed down. From this point on, the relative freedom of touch that one knew as a child is gone. The full use of one of our most basic and most primitive means of communicating is taken from us by society. We can touch our mates and our children, but most other touching behavior is restricted.

Let's consider some of the unwritten societal guidelines for touching behavior in our own culture. Take, for example, the handshake. There are definite rules for the handshake. It must be firm but not too firm, vigorous but not too vigorous, and must not last too long. One may occasionally put an arm around another person, but this generally occurs in times of encouragement, congratulation, or grief.

Why do you scrunch up in a crowded elevator? To avoid touching the other passengers, of course. Frankly it's a good thing that there are numbers above the door to look at; otherwise, we would not even know where to look without feeling invasive. In the United States frequent touching between father and son, friends of the same sex, friends of the opposite sex who are not romantically linked, and the touching of one's own body are frowned upon.

If you look carefully at these unspoken rules and any others you can think of, you will see that they seem to stem from the sexual implications of touching behavior. Somewhere along the way, society has lost the ability to differentiate between physical and sexual behaviors. Touching is physical. It *may or may not* be sexual in nature.

The current cultural norms of touching behavior do much to prevent us from communicating as effectively as we might. They hinder our relationships by keeping people apart. A realization of the importance of touch and an understanding that touching is not necessarily a sexual behavior can do much to open this very important, very basic channel of communication. (A tip: If you tend to have sweaty palms, rub in some violin rosin, which you can carry in your pocket, and that will solve the problem.) Keep in mind, however, that those doing the touching may often be using touch to control a situation.

LOOK . . . DON'T TOUCH . . . SOMETIMES

Research tells us that touching something makes a person more likely to actually select it. If you go to the market and pick up that colorful bag of Ruffles to see just how high the fat and calorie counts are, for example, you're more likely to put the bag in your cart despite the numbers you see. So don't handle anything in the grocery or any other store, unless you're pretty sure you want it to come home with you. The same rationale applies to merchandising techniques that literally hit you where you live. Direct-mail campaigners often stuff their envelopes with bright stickers, glossy coupons and premium offers, and prizes, all to entice you to handle them, with the ultimate intention that you will be manipulated into buying their product or service.

Note that you can use this same information to direct someone else's choice. Let's say you and your husband are trying to decide what color to paint your house. Of the several paint samples before you, you have a clear preference. Instead of pointing

Do you want someone to sit before you do? Then gesture toward the chair . . . they will sit and you are in control.

it out, however, hand it to your husband to make sure that he touches the one you want him to choose. That could very well seal the deal.

Do you want someone to sit before you do? Then gesture toward the chair . . . they will sit and you are in control.

WHO'S THE BOSS?

The next time you are in an adversarial situation, try this: Seat your opponent in a low and very soft chair. You've just put that person at a disadvantage by sitting higher than them and by sitting up straight and alert, not slumped in a poofy chair. Being seated in a low chair will make your adversary feel like a five-year-old. For further advantage, seat him so that the light is in his eyes and behind you. This puts your face in shadow (making you harder to read) and keeps his eyes lowered (because of the glare).

Had your adversary known of these little tricks, he could have easily manipulated the light, chosen a different chair, or moved the chair he was given to a more advantageous angle. Indeed, the very act of asking to move the chair is a form of taking control. But he didn't, and you did. Lucky you.

You have more power over your life and those around you than you think. We all want to influence our boss, for example, especially during disagreements or when trying to get something we want. While you can't make him a robot bending to your every whim, you can manipulate his environment and perceptions, and give yourself the edge.

INCREASE YOUR OFFICE I.Q. (INFLUENCE QUOTIENT)

Sharpen your perception of that environment and you're halfway there. Start by examining your boss's space, both personal and environmental, to see how you can make it work for you.

Personal space: Does he keep a distance when talking to you? Move closer. Invading that personal space a bit will make him feel awkward, and if you're sufficiently subtle, he won't even know why. Holding a pen or your glasses at the same time creates a barrier for you while increasing your own comfort level. While touching is usually a risky proposition, a hand on the shoulder when making a point does provide you with a dominant position.

Initiate the handshake if one is appropriate, and make it strong and short. Don't squeeze—a simple, firm grip palm to palm will do. Again, this provides a subtle signal that you are in charge.

Environmental space: Desks and tables—or even the crossed arms of the person you're talking to—can create physical barriers that translate into barriers to communication. So in his office, put yourself, if possible, on a couch or chair unblocked by his desk. In addition to facilitating the communication, this gives your boss no place to hide. Unless you're seeking a showdown, avoid sitting directly facing him. Sitting diagonally from someone comes across as much friendlier and elicits interaction.

Try to put yourself or an object of yours (a Palm Pilot, Black-Berry, glasses, for example) between him and his phone. Try to leave space between your back and any wall—chairs should not be butted up against the wall. You literally want *his* back against the wall, not yours. Look at the artifacts in the office as though on an archaeological expedition. They will give you clues to weaknesses. Awards on walls may merit comment and appeal to pride. Toys reveal a playful manner. A desk without drawers means an order freak, so make that an example by being even more fastidious.

Conversation: Certain verbal ploys can be used to guide and even manipulate others so that they come around to your point of view. Start out by discovering what the other person's criteria are, and use that to obtain their enthusiastic agreement. Is their criterion spirituality, humor, literacy, financial success? To help, ask yourself these questions:

- What makes this important to them?
- What does this do for them?
- What would I have to do to make them understand me?
- What would have to happen for this person to support my position or request?

Yet, when you are trying to influence people with words, the more you say, the more common you appear and the less in control. Silence is a powerful manipulative tool because it makes others uncomfortable. They feel that they have to fill such voids, which can work to your advantage. Besides, by not being verbose, you will be thought to know much more than perhaps you really do.

When you do speak, using the word "you" will make the other person feel important and clearly the focus of your intentions. "I like working with you." "I admire you." "What do you like to do in your spare time?" I think you get the idea.

You also want to use the voice of authority. Drop the tone on the end of a sentence and people know you mean business. Our parents did it when we were young, our teachers did it when we were older, our bosses do it now. After years of learning this, we respond more to intonation patterns than to meaning, and none of us can avoid being affected. The same thing said in one voice—the voice of authority—turns us into believers, and in another voice into skeptics. As a result, using a firm voice automatically makes us more powerful and influential. We need to practice this, however, because when under stress our voice tone tends to rise, making us sound childish and weak.

Time: We rarely use this tool correctly. Some people think that arriving late demonstrates control. More often than not, however, this tactic backfires because it annoys people. Conversely, coming early puts them on alert—if they are not ready for you, all the better. Have your Palm Pilot to consult or read a journal . . . you can

SEATING CHART

Here's another way you can take advantage of your physical environment to increase the power of influence. Body language provides a variety of clues about ourselves and how we feel about others. We tend to position our bodies according to our feelings about the person we're talking with. Consider how you sit with the following people and what your body is saying about you:

- A counselor (across)
- A lover (next to)
- A child (virtually embracing)
- A stranger (distant and separated)
- An interviewee for a prospective job (forward with interest)

You can use this knowledge about your own tendencies to both read other people and position yourself better in interactions with just about anyone.

use the time productively. For maximum control, also try to set the limit on when a meeting ends. By seeming to have more pressing business, you are in charge. Call it a power play if you will. I prefer to call it a mental strategy that couples your power of suggestion with your mental strength to help you get what you want.

Light: Try to keep a lamp or window behind you. As we saw in the opening example, forcing the boss to look into a light source puts you in the one-up position. If there is a window behind him, bring your chair around catty-corner to his so you're not looking into it, or invite him to join you on the couch.

STYLISH THINKING

You can also improve communication by learning to recognize—and even emulate—someone else's thinking style. Even something as simple as doing what the person to whom you're talking does—when they sit, you sit; when they lean in, you lean in—is a way of showing that you share the same feelings and promotes better empathy and communication. Don't overdo it, though; you want your gestures to say "I think as you think," not "I'm a lunatic copycat."

Making yourself into someone that people can relate to is not the same as manipulating them. Quite the opposite. By giving off the signals you want someone to pick up, and picking up the signals that the other gives off, you are heightening the experience for both of you and turning a blah conversation into a meaningful exchange.

Research suggests that we "think" in terms of our senses, meaning that the information we draw from the world around us is represented in our minds in the form of pictures, sounds, feelings, smells, and tastes. People organize that experience in different ways. We all display thinking preferences at certain times, and therefore differ from others in the ways we perceive and respond to the world around us.

Roughly 45 percent of the population is thought to have a primary preference for thinking in terms of feelings (kinesthetic) compared with 35 percent in terms of visual images and 20 percent in auditory or sound form. A few people even think in terms of smell (olfactory) or taste (gustatory). Recognizing how individuals process thought allows you to fine-tune and adapt your communication to fit their style, which in turn facilitates closer communication and that feeling of synchronicity that makes business deals go well and relationships sing. Conversely, not appreciating these radically different thought processes works against you.

Imagine a conversation between a person thinking visually and a person thinking in feelings. If you're talking about how you feel about things, and somebody else is talking about how they see things, you're talking against each other. One says, "I see the president isn't doing a good job." The other person says, "I feel the president isn't doing the right thing." Believe it or not, you're now talking about two different things. One is literally talking about what he or she has perceived in the news and on the street. The other is reacting emotionally to events.

When I was doing my graduate work, my professor discussed my dissertation with me. I said, "I hear what you're saying." He said, "I don't want you to hear what I'm saying. That means you're not going to do it. *Do* what I'm saying." Even the phrase "I see what you're saying" has a slightly different meaning and tells us how we process our information. I trust my ears more than my eyes, which is why I say, "I hear what you're saying." I had every intention of doing my professor's bidding, whether he thought well of the way I expressed myself or not.

I think early man trusted his ears more than his eyes, too. After all, he had to know so many other things that were going on around him. In many cases, he heard danger before he saw it. Oral traditions, oral cultures, storytelling, myth making, and belief systems all came about through what we told each other, what we experienced through our ears.

This is not to say that there is a right way and a wrong way to interpret the world, only that the knowledge of how you think and how other people think can facilitate better communications. That's key to a win-win negotiation.

The following cues and clues will help guide you in that process.

THINKING IN VISUAL IMAGES

When people do this, they tend to speak more quickly and at a higher pitch. In addition, their breathing may be higher in the chest, which would make it more shallow. There is often an increase in muscle tension, particularly in the shoulders; the head will be up; and the face will often appear paler than normal.

Use strong visual imagery in your requests. "I need that growing pile of papers read and signed on my table by the time the clock shows 10."

These people respond well to diagrams, pictures, seeing a process at work, video, and graphics.

THINKING IN SOUNDS

In this case, people tend to breathe evenly over the whole chest area. You can tell because small rhythmic movements of the body are discernible and voice tonality is clear, expressive, and resonant. The head is well balanced on the shoulders or held slightly at an angle, as if listening to something. Use words that elicit sound . . . be aware of the tone, timbre, and speed of your speech.

To reach these folks, make sure that your verbal instructions are clear and sequential. Music and talk are forms of media of conveying information. They will be easily distracted by noise. "I need the paper by the time the clock strikes 10."

TALKING TO ONESELF

When people do this, they often lean their heads to one side, nestling it on their hand or fist. This is known as the "telephone position," as one gets the impression that they are talking on an invisible telephone. They may actually repeat out loud what they have just "heard," with the result that you can see their lips move.

Verbal repetition accented with repeated visuals is a strong way of getting information to them.

THINKING ABOUT FEELINGS

This is characterized by deep breathing low in the stomach area; that is, the voice has a deeper tonality to it and the individual will typically speak slowly using long pauses. The body language implicit in Rodin's famous sculpture of "The Thinker" could be said to suggest kinesthetic thinking. Talk about how you feel about them doing the job, and use lots of emotion words . . . enjoy, sad, happy, disappoint, angry, etc.

It has also been observed that when we are involved in different kinds of thinking processes, we often gesture toward the sense organ related to it. For example, some people gesture in the direction of their ears while "listening" to sound cues; others may point to their eyes when "visualizing." If we "feel" things particularly strongly, we sometimes gesture toward the abdomen.

These systems of thinking—whether sound-related, feeling-related, or any of the other styles listed above—influence both the choice of words we use in communicating with others and the body language we exhibit. By listening, watching, and asking specific questions, you can tell how people relate to the world and gain considerable insight into their nature. But by listening and looking for dominant thinking styles in others, we reach them on a far clearer level and can take control of the communication process and their reaction to it.

EMOTIONAL THOUGHT

The ability to correctly read individuals' emotions through their nonverbal communication can prove equally helpful. For example, people who are stressed are less in control and thus can be more easily guided or manipulated. If you're a parent, it tells you your child is hiding something. If you're a clergyman or a therapist or a friend, it tells you that you've hit a nerve—a chink in the armor that is probably worth exploring. Being able to recognize someone's tension can also help limit confrontation and actually alleviate that stress.

Professionals who deal with potentially volatile situations, like airline flight crews, are trained to watch for telltale signs of tension, including:

- Repeatedly checking tickets or passports
- Rearranging hand luggage
- Dropping things
- Constantly making last-minute checks
- Changing position in their seats
- Grimacing
- Head scratching
- Earlobe tugging
- Rubbing the back of the neck with the palm of the hand

You can use the same sorts of indicators to spot tension in the people around you every day. Ditto for people suffering from a case of nerves.

Nervousness is a lot like tension, only more so. Performers know all about the jitters: The number one public fear (above being naked in public) is getting up in front of an audience and having to speak. But it doesn't take being in front of a podium—or being naked, for that matter—to make you nervous. Anyone in an uncomfortable situation will experience and display signs of unease: throat-clearing, glancing around the room, rubbing the nose, and jangling money in pockets. Still more nervous gestures include rapid movements, crossing of arms and legs, looking away from other people, moving around and fidgeting when seated, moving toward the edge of a seat rather than relaxing into it, playing with objects, chain-smoking, and pointing your body toward the nearest exit. All these things are quite normal, simple, and important to spot.

Stress is the great killer of Americans today. It leads to hardening of the arteries and heart attacks. It also leads to unclear thinking and to anger and conflict, which in turn cause more stress. We live in a society where everything is pushing down on us—the clock is ticking, we have deadlines, children, payments, and unending other responsibilities. Physiologically, we are not built for this sort of thing. Multi-tasking, which most of us do out of necessity, is a joke. This isn't to say that the guy being chased by saber-toothed tigers didn't have his own stress. Chances are he died young and didn't have a good life either, but if we're living longer and talking about having a good life, you want to eliminate stress as much as possible. That's the one thing most of us neglect, even when we're told over and over how important it is.

After a major seminar I had run about recognizing and reducing stress in cardiac patients at Jacoby Hospital in the Bronx, one of the cardiologists came up to me.

"I have a patient who I know is going to have a heart attack and he doesn't listen to a thing that I say," he told me.

"Is this the kind of person that you are being sweet to and he misses appointments?" I asked.

"Yeah," he replied.

"But in your gut you feel he's just not taking your advice?"

"No, he doesn't listen. He keeps on with his lifestyle."

To me, it was clear that the doctor had to take a new approach. "Scare the guy," I told him. "Tell him, 'If you don't stop the way you are living now, within a month, you will be dead.'" I believe those words saved that man's life.

Relaxation techniques are effective ways to overcome stress. Practice the ones in this book, and you'll not only develop a master mind but you'll also live longer to enjoy it.

Though not the killer that stress is, fear is even easier to recognize because the intensity of the emotion exaggerates our reactions. When we are frightened, our eyes open wide, even stare, as if we need to take in more of the scene before us. They'll frequently dart about as we desperately seek a way out of the situation. Often pale when faced with a frightening situation, some people may merely tense up, ready for a fight. Those of us who are less assertive will most definitely run away. Either way, our bodies' sudden production of adrenaline will make our muscles rigid, often to the point of trembling, and speed up our heart and breathing rates.

MISCUES AND MISINTERPRETATIONS

Recognizing someone's emotional or psychological state, and reacting to it appropriately, is a surefire way to enhance communication, as long as your own body language conveys the proper message in return. Just as emotions can make or break our experience of the world at any given time and place, so can the miscommunication of those emotions when our body language—our nonverbal cues—are misinterpreted.

Newscasters, for example, sometimes smile at the close of reporting a horrifying story. This is not a reason to be angry with the newscaster, or anyone else who displays an inappropriate expression, including those people who smile or laugh at funerals. These reactions are merely unconscious responses to situations, a way of projecting, "I don't know what face to wear here."

My youngest son used to smile whenever he got in trouble at school. That was his way of expressing discomfort and projecting his good intentions. His teachers and the principal, however, read that smile as the smirk of the unrepentant smart aleck, which didn't help him one bit when it came to getting back in their good graces. By videotaping my son's affective display and then playing it back for him to see, I was able to help him straighten out his misread cues before the situation deteriorated any further.

You could very well be sending similarly misconstrued cues whenever you need some time to be by yourself. Can't we all say in a campy Swedish accent, "*I vant to be alone*"? These necessary periods during which we recharge our mental batteries, called *downtime*, can be as quick as a 10-second deep breath or as lengthy as days of solitary contemplation. No matter how long or short, you send out unmistakable nonverbal signals in order to carve out this space for yourself. You will possibly tilt your head away from other people, look aside from time to time, shift your shoulders at an angle but not actively turn away. This body language clearly states that you're in your own world, whether conjuring up a specific memory or simply engaged in personal reflections. If, on the other hand, you opt to stand or sit in a position where people cannot talk to you, they will not only leave you alone right then and there but they'll start to avoid you entirely, feeling that you have no time for them at all.

Sadly, this unintentional dismissal of people is often to blame when people say they "know" that others don't like them. Their own behavior, which is quite marked, provokes the very reactions that make them so unhappy. To make matters worse, these individuals further handicap themselves through their conversational styles. Convinced that any discussion will prove difficult, they become awkward when conversing, often talking in short sentences, grunting, and becoming monosyllabic. A detrimental brew of low self-esteem mixed with the feeling of being disliked propels these types to radiate aggression with their behavior. By coming across as angry, rather than shy or nervous, they've created a self-fulfilling prophecy—the realized expectation of bad things happening and of being socially ostracized.

A similar scenario exists with those who are pessimistic. Optimists create a receptive framework by being outgoing, smiling, hospitable, and friendly. That attitude creates opportunities for conversation and friendship, as well as creating positive outcomes to situations. Conversely, concentrating on the more negative aspects produces a negative behavior pattern.

In short, body language not only speaks for us but it can also shape our reality. One 75-year-old man I know routinely walks with his head down and his shoulders slumped. Though he is in reality physically active and intellectually engaged, his posture says otherwise. The notion is reinforced by the greeting on his telephone answering machine, in which his voice lowers instead of rising at the last word or syllable of each sentence. Try reading aloud the following telephone greeting, letting your voice drop on the syllables written in bold. *Hello. This is Joe **Blow**. Please leave a message at the **tone**.* What a downer, right? That's a total misrepresentation of the man, and probably of you, too. That cheerless phone message, along with the one he communicates with every step, creates a less than uplifting advertisement for him, one that doesn't begin to get him what he wants out of life.

MENTAL INFLUENCE MINDSCRIPT

Building your confidence is an essential part of gaining the advantage when dealing with people. Let's face it, no one puts much stock in a Self-Doubting Thomas. This mindscript will help build your confidence.

What's Not to Like?

Close your eyes and allow yourself gently to relax.

Scan your memories and identify any time in your life when you felt confident.

Allow yourself to travel back to that experience. Relive it in your mind and get a sense of those feelings you felt then. Explore and enjoy that positive time once more in your mind.

When you can experience that confident feeling, close your dominant hand into a tight fist. As you do this, allow those feelings of confidence to increase. That fist can represent your inner determination to be that more confident person.

As you clench your fist tighter still, allow that feeling of confidence to spread out and touch every part of you. The deeper part of your mind can memorize this marvelous feeling.

Repeatedly give yourself the suggestion that, in future, whenever you close your dominant hand into a tight fist in this way you can once more enjoy this feeling of confidence. You can also suggest that you can be pleasantly surprised at how long afterward this positive feeling can remain with you.

Relax and open that fist, allowing yourself to drift into an even more comfortable state.

Before completing your exercise, make that hand into a tight fist of confidence again and notice how once more that positive memory and that confident feeling can come flowing through.

The more you practice this exercise, the stronger that association between clenching your fist and feeling confident can become. Knowing there is something you can do to increase your feeling of confidence in any situation can in itself increase your confidence still further. Learn to understand and build on your strengths and abilities. None of us is perfect, but we can strive to be the very best we can be.

APPEARANCES CAN BE REVEALING

Studies of body language have shown that people display a range of six emotions—sadness, happiness, anger, disgust, fear, and surprise—that cross all boundaries (gender, age, race, and nationality). How many of those have you experienced in the last week alone? Most, I'd bet. And as much as you'd probably like to think that you effectively camouflaged the majority of those feelings, in all likelihood you didn't.

Join the crowd. Try as we may to mask how we feel, especially when attempting to keep that stiff upper lip that's supposed to be so admirable, our emotions almost always register in our nonverbal

MIND BUILDER

Those mental muscles have been getting a workout. You now have power over others, simply by the way you stand, talk (or don't talk), gesture, and move. Use this test to see how well you can use external cues to make appropriate deductions about someone's internal makeup.

Go inside a stranger's office and study the room as though you were an archaeologist. What's on the walls? Check out the desk. Do you see toys, clear space, photos? Are the papers filed or piled? Be quick about this step, so you don't get caught. Jot clues down in the chart below. You might even bring a Polaroid camera and snap some shots so you can take off even faster. And don't bother to call me if you are apprehended—I will disavow all knowledge of your activities.

Once you're no longer technically trespassing, use the clues to construct in your mind the characteristics of the person whose office this is. What is this person saying, whether intentionally or not, about him- or herself through the office décor, artifacts, clutter, or lack of it? Then find someone who actually knows that person and note how accurate you were.

cues. With the right knowledge, however, you can manipulate your nonverbal cues so that they build you up instead of tear you down.

Find yourself a pair of glasses, even if they are only clear glass inside a frame. Make sure they are stylish, and use them as a way to make your gestures more emphatic when you wish to make a point. Research shows that, for whatever reason, people with glasses are perceived as bright. So wear them and, once the impression is gained, take them off. Rumor has it that a top CNN newscaster wears glasses with plain glass just to look a bit more intellectual.

On the verbal front, you can even appear infinitely intelligent,

	Clues	Characteristics	Accuracy
Example	Messy desk	Disorganized	Yes—loses files
Example	Boat painting	Outdoorsman, sailor	No—painting was his dad's
1			
2			
3			
4			
5			
6			
7			
8			
9			
10			

always a help when trying to impress or win over others, by what you don't say. That may sound like a contradiction but it's not. As we discussed earlier, the number one rule for appearing intelligent is simple: silence. Silence creates an aura of deep thought. If you're not talking, you must just be holding back something of great wisdom or depth. When you choose to speak, make sure to agree with one of the other person's points. But don't say "uh-huh." Instead, respond with a brisk "sure," meaning that you knew all this already and were merely being reminded of it.

You can't be silent or monosyllabic forever. So when you do speak, stare at a spot on the other person's forehead, directly between their eyes. This gives the impression that you are literally transmitting your thoughts into their consciousness. Keep your speech direct, almost to the point of terseness. You want to create the illusion that you could say much more, but that you simply choose not to expound.

In addition, you can subtly imply that you are impatient for the conversation to end. Let people know you have other things on your mind: Tap your fingers on a table surface while awaiting responses from others, or steeple your fingers. This is a classic subliminal cue denoting both impatience and superiority.

The clincher? Read the *New York Times Book Review* bestseller list. It provides titles and synopses of all the current literature, everything you need to know to participate in a conversation intelligently. When asked if you've read any book, reply only, "Well, not in English."

Using your verbal power in tiny doses can reap huge benefits. You've shown that you can reflect a person's thinking style and that you can listen (that's flattering as well as intelligence-boosting).

INSTANT BRAIN POWER

To take things one step further, almost into the realm of hypnosis, you need to use words even more selectively. By merely emphasizing certain words in a sentence, you can influence the other person into doing exactly what you want.

You don't believe me? Then try this exercise. Ask a partner to pick a number between 1 and 4. Have them write down the number they immediately think of. You can impress them by writing the number "3"—keeping it shielded from their view, of course— before you even ask the question. Statistically, most people pick 3. Besides, you can give them a little mind-push by phrasing the question like this: *Pick a number from one to four.* This way, you have

MIND BUILDER

Mental power and persuasion rely heavily on accurate anticipation. The next time you sit down in front of a movie, try to second-guess the next scene or bit of dialogue.

mentioned all the numbers between 1 and 4—"from one to (2) four"—except 3, and their minds will fill in the blanks.

Here is another good example of the human capacity for accepting an idea and responding to it almost automatically. Tell a friend that you see he has a scratch on his arm. Ask, "Does it itch?" He will probably deny both the wound and the sensation. But persist, looking at his arm more intently. Don't give up. Eventually he will scratch. The implications are known by every stage hypnotist. You cannot ignore most verbal and physical suggestions, if delivered in a confident manner. A cough, eyes misting up, or yawn often gets a parallel response. In terms of scratching, a performer may say the itching sensations are all over your body, the neck, the shoulders, and they are getting more and more itchy . . . and you can't help yourself from scratching. You want proof this works . . . you are in all likelihood scratching while reading these words.

Here's another easy way to impress those around you with your mental prowess. Ask a partner to imagine two children fighting, hitting each other. Ask them, "Are the children boys?" Most people will say yes.

We can implant some tendencies in people's minds by accenting or leaving the choice for last. "Do you want this week or *next week off*?" "Think carefully before *you give me the money*" or "decide not to *pay me*."

Because they are embedded, these kinds of subliminal com-

7 WAYS TO CREATE A POWERFUL IMAGE
IN YOUR OFFICE

Yes, your office should be comfortable and familiar, but it's not a game room. A burl-walnut executive clock? Good. Your tattered John Riggins poster? Bad. Your goal is to surround yourself with stuff that says, "I'm the one who's really in charge here, but let's not make a big deal about it, okay?" Here are seven office must-haves.

1. **Your Diploma** It demonstrates ability, pride, and confidence. Don't give it center stage, though—just tuck it away in a corner somewhere to show you're modest, too.
2. **A Family Photo** It defines who you are, and—more important—gives you license to throw your weight around a bit. You must possess redeeming qualities, after all, if the hot wife and cute kid still love you.
3. **A Dumbbell** Set it on the floor in full view. It says to your coworkers, "I take my health as seriously as the company's."
4. **A Map or Globe** It demonstrates interest in world events, which implies that you're a big-picture thinker.

mands do not create as much resistance as simply saying them might.

You can emphasize or mark certain words in your sentence in a variety of ways that don't even involve speech. In addition to saying them more loudly or more softly,

> To know and use someone's name often creates an almost magical state of control and attention.

look the other person in the eye only as you say those words that comprise your command. Alternately, you can nod your head, or

5. **A Signed Anything** A painting, photo, baseball. It conveys importance through association.
6. **A Set of Something** Encyclopedias, rare books, whatever. It shows you have a focused and curious mind.
7. **A Ticking Clock** It says, "I'm important and busy. Make this quick."

AND 6 THAT SUGGEST WEAKNESS...

1. **An Ashtray** How can you control your corner of the company if you can't control your nicotine craving?
2. **Tube TV** Your ideas are probably outdated, too.
3. **Formica Furniture** You're not even important enough for wood? So sorry.
4. **A Candy-Colored Computer** Maybe you ought to showcase your creativity through your work instead.
5. **Cardboard Boxes** Going somewhere?
6. **Anything Orange** It suggests emotional instability or an overactive something.

even open your eyes wider or close them sleepily as you utter the words you want someone to act on.

The one word you don't need to emphasize but you do need to use is the other person's name. To know and use someone's name often creates an almost magical state of control and attention.

Have trouble remembering names? Read on as I share how to power up your mind and your memory in the next chapter.

PART 2

SOFTWARE KEYS— GAMES PEOPLE PLAY (IMP)

CHAPTER 6

YOUR INTUITION KNOWS (KEY 4)

SOLVE PROBLEMS BY FINDING THE ANSWER INSIDE

In most interviews with newspapers and television, I credit much of my mental ability to a combination of reading nonverbal behavior and accessing intuitions. By this point, you should now be well trained in the nonverbal. Now comes the *coup de grâce*.

Intuition is the small voice that advises you based on everything you have picked up and processed in your life. There are physicians who can shake your hand and know what's wrong with you. They're not psychic, they're not supernatural. They're simply picking up certain moisture in your palm, ruddiness in your cheek, a drooping eyebrow, and then integrating that subconsciously with all the medical knowledge they possess to diagnose your illness. They may not even know how they are accessing their information. That is the power of intuition.

Whether you're a parent, a lover, or a businessperson, by becoming aware of your intuition and insight, you can enhance those skills and solve professional and personal quandaries more easily than you ever thought possible by finding the answers inside yourself.

A primitive skill that early humans relied upon to survive, intuition recombines all of our sensory input with "a sixth sense," a transcendental insight or a feeling in the gut. Your intuition is not some strange, separate entity, but rather a part of you that you can rely on, if you only give it a chance. Though we're taught to rely on rational thought, we use the power of our intuition every day without realizing it. We also ignore it to our detriment.

You need to pay attention to that voice inside. If you're walking someplace and you have a feeling that you shouldn't go there, don't go there. If somebody seems like someone you want to get to know better, do it. If you feel that you should go to bed instead of trying to crank out that report, hit the sack and get up early.

Sometimes, it's hard to hear that intuitive voice. The father of a friend of mine had decided to move to a new city and was trying to choose between buying a lot and building a house, or buying a house he had seen and fallen in love with. Though he felt torn, what he really wanted seemed clear to his daughter. Every time he spoke of the house, he talked about how perfect it was for him, how he could see himself there. Every time he mentioned the lot, he talked in terms of "should" and potential gain, along with the dread he felt at the idea of a year of construction. His intuition was speaking loud and clear. Like many of us, he just hadn't learned how to listen.

You can become increasingly aware of your intuitive side by simply exercising those particular mental muscles.

Next time you're at a bank of elevators, see if you can intuit which one is going to arrive next.

As you're coming out of a sleep state in the morning, see if you can get any impressions about the day's news. (No fair cheating with the news on your clock radio.)

Try to name who is on the phone when it rings. (Caller I.D. doesn't count!)

Try to see if you can intuit some of the headlines for the next week, month, or year. And keep a list in your intuition journal, PDA, or spreadsheet.

Pay attention to what you intuit about the business trends in your industry this year.

Play a guessing game with your radio or TV. "Name that tune" *before* you turn on your radio, or the next video on an MTV rotation. You may be surprised at how often you get it right! My wife, Tova, correctly predicted each of eight songs sung by Paul Simon in a live set on public television. Not to try is certainly to fail.

Any time you find yourself getting one of these everyday occurrences right, give yourself a pat on the back for tuning in on target. Positive engenders positive.

There are two pencil drawings on page 225. They are of something outside. My kids came up with them. Without over thinking, but going intuitive, what do you think they are?

How well did you do? Why did you go in that direction? What cues led your thinking and allowed you to intuit it? Open yourself to the possibility, and have fun with it.

Masaru Ibuka, founder and former chief advisor of Sony, was known to mull integral decisions over a cup of herbal tea. Based on his body's response to the tea (which he read as his gut reaction), he would settle on a resolution.

WANT MORE PROOF THAT YOU SHOULD LISTEN TO YOUR GUT?

In a recent article in *Science* (February 2006, Volume 311), Ap Dijksterhuis is talking about consumer intuition and its direct connection to consumer behavior. When the time comes to decide, go with what feels right. "It is much better to follow your gut," said Dijksterhuis, a professor of psychology at the University of Amsterdam, who led the research entitled "On Making the Right Choice: The Deliberation-Without-Attention Effect."

In one experiment, students were asked to pick one of four cars based on a list of positive and negative attributes. A description of each car's attributes was flashed on a computer screen for 8 seconds, according to the paper.

First, the experimenters provided a simple choice, where each car had a list of just four attributes, some positive ("has good mileage") and some negative ("has poor leg room"). Half of the students were asked to think about their choice for 4 minutes. The other half were asked to do challenging, distracting puzzles for 4 minutes, preventing them from consciously considering the car options.

In this experiment, the conscious thinkers did a better job than the distracted students of selecting the best car, which was the only one with three positive characteristics; other cars in the experiment had fewer.

Next, the researchers did a similar experiment, but with a much more complicated choice: Each car was described with a list of 12 attributes rather than the four in the prior test. This time the students who were not allowed to think consciously about the decision did a better job of selecting the car with the most positive attributes.

The results seem to state that if there are too many variables, it's better for the unconscious mind to rationalize and integrate the data into a coherent picture and make a better choice. Listen to your gut!

"The crazier the times are, the more important it is for leaders to develop and to trust their intuition," suggests management guru Tom Peters. Once thought of as the domain of the "gifted few," intuition is, in fact, readily available to us all. It can be an important component in making hiring decisions, motivating staff, increasing sales, accessing partnerships, and predicting industry trends.

In today's fast-paced environment, decisions need to be made swiftly and accurately. While many top executives won't publicize it, intuition is a key part of their decision-making success. A classic but unverifiable study by executive search firm Christian &

Timbers showed that, among 601 executives at Fortune 1,000 companies, 55 percent perceive that they base their decisions on facts and figures, while 45 percent say they rely more heavily on their intuition.

Roy Rowan, author of *The Intuitive Manager*, states, "Logic and analysis can lead a person only partway down the path to a profitable decision. The last step to success frequently requires a daring intuitive leap." Intuition is the secret weapon of many successful leaders. They describe it as knowing something directly without going through a long analytical process.

And how about these findings in the *Journal of Advanced Nursing* (Volume 26, Page 194—July 1997) in an article titled "Intuition: a critical review of the research and rhetoric" by L. King and J.V. Appleton: "The point is research evidence suggests that intuition occurs in response to knowledge, is a trigger for action and/or reflection and thus has a direct bearing on analytical processes in patient/client care. The authors therefore argue that the essential nature of intuition cannot be ignored in the practice, management, education and research of nursing."

Gary Kasparov can play and beat the best chess computer. How is this possible when the computer can calculate positions many moves further ahead than he can? It is because of his intuitive grasp of the game. Experience allows him to combine analysis with a "sense" of which move is best.

Additional examples of intuition in strategic decision making are all around us. Ignoring recommendations from advisors, Ray Kroc purchased the McDonald's brand from the McDonald brothers. As he said in his autobiography, *Grinding It Out*, "I'm not a gambler and I didn't have that kind of money, but my funny bone instinct kept urging me on."

Ignoring numerous naysayers and a lack of supporting market research, Bob Lutz, former president of Chrysler, made the Dodge Viper a reality:

"It was this subconscious, visceral feeling. And it just felt right." (*Forbes*, 1989)

Ignoring the fact that 24 publishing houses had rejected the book and her own publishing house was opposed, Eleanor Friede gambled on a "little nothing book" called *Jonathan Livingston Seagull*: "I felt there were truths in this simple story that would make it an international classic. It was groundbreaking."

Successful entrepreneurs are more intuitive in their cognitive style than the general population of managers (*European Journal of Work and Organizational Psychology*, Volume 9, Number 1, March 1, 2000).

Albert Einstein, the great logician of our times, paid many a tribute to intuition. Among the most telling: "Imagination is more important than knowledge."

> Successful entrepreneurs are more intuitive in their cognitive style than the general population of managers (*European Journal of Work and Organizational Psychology*, Volume 9, Number 1, March 1, 2000).

"The intuitive mind is a sacred gift and the rational mind is a faithful servant. We have created a society that honors the servant and has forgotten the gift."

Inj Jadish Parikh, in *Intuition: The New Frontier in Management* (Blackwell, London, 1994), conducted a survey of 1,312 managers in nine countries. He found almost 80 percent admitted to using intuition and believe that it contributes to corporate success and more than 70 percent believe that intuition also is important to R&D efforts.

These managers listed several definitions of intuition. The most common were nonlogical thinking, decisions without reason, decisions based on few clues or data points, a feeling from within, subconscious analysis derived from information stored in memory, a gut feeling, a sixth sense, and spontaneous knowing. Almost 60 percent believe that intuition can be enhanced. I believe that intuitive abilities can be enhanced in everyone.

WHERE IS YOUR INTUITION?

It seems that intuition emerges from the subconscious. A successful CEO correctly analyzes a situation faster than a top MBA student. The CEO draws upon a wealth of information stored in the memories. The brain gathers information stored in memory and "packages" it as a new insight or solution. The successful CEO only experiences the intuition; the work is done in the subconscious.

Hotel magnate Conrad Hilton was known for his hunches. During a sealed bidding process for the Stevens Corporation, for example, Hilton entered his first bid at $165,000. "Somehow that didn't feel right to me," he said about the incident. "Another figure kept coming, $180,000. It satisfied me. It seemed fair. It felt right. I changed my bid to the larger figure on that hunch." Hilton's bid proved to be the highest—but by only $200! His intuition won the bid and eventually netted him more than $2 million on this one deal.

Hilton himself described how his intuitive process worked—first he would work through all the logical planning of a problem, then wait for an internal response. "When I have a problem and have done all I can to figure it, I keep listening in a sort of inside silence 'til something clicks and I feel the right answer," he explained.

Plenty of others have discovered the power of listening to their intuition. Roy Rowan of *Fortune* magazine conducted surveys and interviews among the CEOs of Fortune 500 companies and found that the vast majority not only believed in intuition but they also admitted to using it in their business careers. According to many of Mr. Rowan's sources, intuition can be nurtured and even taught. "More than half of the Fortune 500 companies, including Procter & Gamble, IBM, Shell, and Singer, have undertaken some kind of creativity experiments or training," he writes. He quotes Eugene Gendlin, a University of Chicago psychology professor, as saying that executives can be taught to recognize and interpret the physical sensations that an idea elicits. "You can train people so they have the capacity to get a hunch anytime they want one," Mr. Gendlin says. Mr. Rowan says that "the biggest winners tomorrow will be those who can summon from somewhere deep inside themselves glimpses of the economic landscape ahead and intuitive flashes of the business opportunities that have yet to surface."

The *Harvard Business Review*, Landry, J. (2003), reviews "Intuition at work: why developing your gut instincts will make you better at what you do", Vol. 81 No.2, pp.22., and reports that corporate executives found that successful, high-ranking managers operating under stress and pressure constantly relied on hunches and feelings when faced with complex problems. The research concluded, as we saw with Conrad Hilton, that managers could be most successful by combining logic with intuition.

Take the following story. It owes as much to reasoning and memory as it does to intuition. The mix makes a potent brew when it comes to making mental connections.

A Jewish scholar living in Russia wanted to visit Moscow. After much negotiation, which dragged on for months, he was granted permission. Boarding the train, he found a seat in an empty compartment. At the next station a young man entered the compartment and sat down.

The scholar looked at the young man and thought: "Well, he doesn't look like a peasant but he probably comes from this district. Now this is a Jewish district so therefore he must be Jewish. On the other hand, I am the only one from our district who has permission to go to Moscow, so where could this man be going? Ah, just outside Moscow there is a little village called Samvet, and it doesn't require special permission to visit there.

"But why is he going to Samvet? He must be going to visit one of the Jewish families there but now there are only two. The Botvinniks and the Steinbergs. The Botvinniks stay pretty much to themselves and don't like guests, so he must be visiting the Steinbergs.

"But why? The Steinbergs have only girls, so maybe he is their son-in-law. But if so, which daughter did he marry? Esthi married the nice lawyer from Budapest, and Bluma married a businessman from Zamodir and moved to America, so it must be Esthi's husband. Now if I am not mistaken, his name is Sender Shimon. But he comes from Budapest; they are very anti-Semitic there, so he must have changed his name. What's the Hungarian equivalent of Shimon? Szymync! But if they let him change his name, he must have some special status. What could it be? A doctorate from the university."

At this point the scholar turns to his fellow traveler and says, "How do you do, Dr. Szymync?"

"Very well, thank you," declared the surprised passenger, "but how do you happen to know my name?"

"Oh," replied the scholar, "it was obvious."

The scholar's conclusion resulted from a logical mental process. He must have read this book! First he noted nonverbal details that others might have missed. Then he remembered people's names and backgrounds. Finally, he bolstered those facts with reasoned intuition and made the connections that led to his conclusion. By tapping this set of mental skills, he looks like a genius, and his mental feat looks like magic.

Does that sound like the kind of process you go through when you're trying to decide whether to make scrambled eggs or an omelette? The idea here is to elevate that humble inner voice and encourage it to speak up on the bigger issues in your life. Not that I think the eggs-versus-omelette question is trivial, just that your basic multi-million dollar contract negotiations might benefit from the same inner consultation.

PLUGGING INTO THE PROCESS

Your mind thinks more or less in pictures and images, not words. That's its natural form. Words have to be learned. Pictures do not. You can use that to access your intuition and problem-solve. If I asked you to close your eyes and describe your bedroom, a picture of that room would pop into your mind's eye. The furniture, curtains, and bed linen would most definitely not appear as words or letters of the alphabet. Frequently, the images in your mind will elicit certain feelings or emotions in you. An image of a tree in a field may bring a memory of a picnic from years ago—a cherished childhood memory. On the other hand, if someone you knew was struck by lightning while standing under a tree in a thunderstorm, it might elicit a totally different emotion.

While these mental images are most often neutral, each is laden with a message. Surely you must have had the experience of talking with someone, and something they said triggered an entirely different thought in your mind? By harnessing these images, you can milk your subconscious and trigger your intuition.

FIND THE ANSWERS INSIDE

Before we go any further, we need to establish a few basics to make sure we're speaking the same language. When I am talking about the logical mind, I am referring to the conscious, reasoning, analytical part, which thinks in fragments and is both judgmental and linear. The subconscious is the inner you, your dreams. It holds all the experiences you have ever had. This truly intuitive side is expansive, non-judgmental, and detached, and provides infinite intelligence for us to tap into. This is where all knowledge already exists. For practical purposes, when I say use your intuitive side, or "let go," your mind will be employing either or both the subconscious and the inner mind. It does not matter from where the answer or inspiration comes. What matters is that you get to it.

Let's set up a hypothetical situation. Your grandfather dies. You know he's left a will. You have absolutely no idea where he hid it. It's not in his safety deposit box or any of the other logical places. So you ask yourself the question of the day, "Where did Grandpa hide the will?" As soon as you've voiced your inquiry, let images flow through your mind, one thing leading to another, whether logical or not.

Assume that in response to the question "Where did Grandpa hide the will?" the image of an ice cream truck comes into your mind. As you allow your mind to wander, you notice that the truck has large promotions for Eskimo pies on its side. This makes you think of that box of Bjork records in the cellar, or the freezer in the attic. It's a start—those are places where you should begin looking for the will.

We know more than we think we do. And we can do more with that knowledge than we ever imagined.

James Watt worked long and hard on how to make engine parts rotate smoothly, but he wasn't any nearer to solving his problem. One night he dreamed of molten metal fragments falling from the sky and forming into globes as they cooled. That vision inspired the manufacture of ball bearings.

Elias Howe spent several years inventing the sewing machine. One small detail was still missing, but he couldn't figure out the solution, until the night he dreamed that he'd been captured by a tribe of savages whose leader insisted he finish his invention or be killed. As he was being led away to be killed, he noticed the spears carried by the savages had eye-shaped holes near the flattened points. Upon awakening, he made a needle with a hole nearer the point, rather than in the middle. This final piece of the puzzle formed the basis for the modern sewing machine.

In understanding deeper principles, intuition operates as a faculty that allows us to synthesize. As Albert Einstein said, "There are no logical paths to these laws; only intuition resting on sympathetic understanding of experience can reach them." Discoveries in chemistry, physics, and other fields have been attributed to intuition. The discoverers of the double-helix structure of DNA were said to have dreamed about that twisted ladder structure before actually proving its existence. Einstein performed what he called "thought experiments" where he would visualize himself in a certain situation and then analyze the outcome. What would happen if I rode a bike at the speed of light? What would happen to the bike, to me, to the sounds, to the light?

Economist John Maynard Keynes said of Isaac Newton: "It was his intuition which was pre-eminently extraordinary. So happy in his conjectures that he seemed to know more than he could possibly have any hope of proving. The proofs were dressed up afterwards; they were not the instrument of discovery."

A very young Walt Disney discovered the concepts of cartoon animation in his daydreams. He also spoke of a small mouse that appeared in his nocturnal dreams. This same pathway is open to all of us. With a little practice, you too can let your subconscious work on a tricky problem or on an important decision while you are awake or calmly snoring away, since dreams provide us with nightly feedback about what is really happening in our lives.

While you can mix and match any of the tools and methods presented in this chapter, since you're probably most interested in the easy route, I'll give you my six steps to successful intuitive thought without further ado:

1. Tell yourself before you go to bed that you will remember your dreams.
2. Before you go to bed, ask yourself the question you want solved. Be as specific and concise as possible.
3. Avoid stimulants for a couple of hours before bed. Tea, coffee,

and cocoa all contain caffeine; even alcohol isn't as conducive to sweet slumber as you might expect. Instead, take a relaxing soak in a hot bath to relieve any physical tension. Quiet baroque music in the background also helps.

4. Before retiring, if you have the time, briefly record your day's activities in a journal kept by your bed. Even more important, record your thoughts or feelings about these activities and events. Then write down the question you are asking yourself.

5. Just before you get into the bed, tell yourself that you will sleep soundly, awaken refreshed, and that you will remember your dream. (Remember that self-programming material we discussed earlier?)

6. When you do wake up, access your mind to retrieve the images from your dream. Like one hanging thread that when pulled unravels an entire garment, one small clue will give you the whole picture, and lead you right through the rest of the dream.

Now you have to interpret what you have, unraveling the strands or blowing away the clouds. Start by giving your dream a title, as though it were a movie. Use as few words as possible. What is the theme of your dream? Summarize it in a sentence or less. What are the major symbols in your dream? What seems to stick out most in your mind? Is it hiding something? What are your feelings? You don't have to be Sigmund Freud to discern the meaning of your dream. The most obvious answer, the one your intuition points to, is usually the right one. Trust yourself to get it right.

ALL-AROUND HELPER

Your world throws opportunities at you. With your heightened sense of awareness and your keener intuition, you will become aware of opportunities that you never knew existed.

Intuition is an invaluable faculty for making major life decisions, such as:

- Deciding to move abroad or to a new house
- Entering into a business partnership or deciding whom you should marry
- Assessing the worth in investment of time in undertaking long-term projects
- Evaluating people such as job applicants or a defendant in a court
- Accepting or rejecting opportunities in life such as promotion, trips, etc.

Oftentimes, we overemphasize rationalization, facts, reason, and logic. Logic and analyses, however, can only take you so far. Luckily, you don't have to rely on a trip to dreamland to enlist your subconscious. For example, you may hesitate to accept one job possibility because another even better job is about to become available somewhere else, maybe at a level or company that you never dreamed you'd have a shot at. This takes us back to that old adage that I will keep sending your way: Trust your intuition.

But if you're really restless, here's something you can do to get some answers about what you think, feel, dream, and imagine. Ready for this amazing advice? Here goes. If all else fails, flip a coin. Not what you were expecting to hear, huh? Well, try it anyway.

Think about the decision you're trying to make. Form it in your mind as a yes or no question. "Should I take the job with Big Gizmo Corporation?"

"Should I apply to graduate school now?" "Should I stop dating John?"

Take a coin and flip it. Heads indicates yes. Tails indicates no. Okay, what was the answer?

But wait! There's more to this exercise.

Think about how you felt about the answer. Were you disappointed? Relieved? Did you get a thrill of excitement through your body or a knot of fear in your stomach? Admit it, did you immediately want to flip the coin two more times and try for best two out of three? (Or have you actually done that already?)

Any of these responses is a demonstration of your intuition speaking to you. Your response gave you information about the answer to your decision. So often we expect our intuition to be a booming God-like voice saying, "BERNIE: TAKE THAT JOB AT BIG GIZMO CORPORATION!"

It's more likely to speak through subtle feelings, inner nudges, or physical sensations. When you learn to pay attention and act on these responses, they can be just as loud and clear as that booming voice.

It all gets down to practice, so when you're in the heat of battle, when you need it, your intuition will be there for you. Keep trying, even when you're at a loss.

INTUITION JOURNAL

I am not a big fan of journals, but this is reasonably painless and does help keep track of the intuitive growth. Use a spreadsheet on your laptop or a Treo if you wish, or send it as an e-mail to yourself on your BlackBerry; just try to keep a record.

By forcing awareness each day, you'll begin to see how often you receive intuitive information. I used to write down the first four thoughts I had during the day and see how many popped up during the day. These things could have been as basic as "torn red sock," or the name "Anne" or "xxx." And suddenly, at some point in the day, somebody would take off a sneaker at a bus stop and they'd have a torn red sock. Was I looking for that torn red sock? Was it self-fulfilling prophecy? It doesn't matter. What it did was to tune me to pay attention to things around me.

Here are a few tips to help you get started on your intuition record. I want to help you keep accurate notes while charting your progress. You'll be amazed someday when you look back at how far you've come!

Record synchronicities and coincidences. Sometimes the information you record will not seem immediately important. In retrospect you may see that you had a predictive experience.

Don't edit or censor the information you receive. You learn as much from your failures as you do from your successes. Also, time may tell you that you were more right than you could ever imagine. And mistakes will happen. There are dates that seem like a good idea at the time and then turn out terribly, food that was purchased with the highest hopes of a delicious meal that winds up tasting like sawdust. Life is full of these disappointments, but they're a total waste of time if we don't learn from them.

Aside from the big picture, make sure that you're taking care of the small stuff, too. Do your research on any decision you need to be making. Exercise so your thoughts and energy flow. Go on a walk through your neighborhood so you see a different view of the reality that surrounds you. Dance, jump, smell the coffee. Have fun.

Keep in mind that you're still learning. You're learning patience with yourself as well as patience with your circumstances. Remember that everything takes time.

Many facts and forces may need to come into play before the path becomes clear. So as you read through newspapers and magazines, cut out pictures, headlines, articles that catch your eye, especially if they are not in your normal field of interest. Keep these clippings with your intuition journal. Write the date on the back of the piece of newspaper or article. Over time you will notice underlying trends. These trends will recall messages from your subconscious.

There is no precise way to understand your intuitive messages. You have to decide what they mean to you. You will need to read them over and use your logical mind to interpret them. As you go over them, one part may jump out at you and that will be the answer. One image may suggest something completely different, perhaps an association from your childhood, which suggests an activity that is your answer. The main thing is you will know. Your inner being will react and say, "Yes, that's it." As you ponder your notes, just allow the answer to come to you.

INTUITING THOUGHTS

Part of tapping into intuition is the ability to see things from someone else's point of view. When I was developing a segment for my first television special, I had artist Peter Max stand on top of one of the World Trade towers while I stood on the other. As the cameras rolled, Peter was asked to make a drawing on a canvas. My job was to duplicate it.

High above the urban canyons of the city (today the memory of what was lost still sends shivers through me), I felt both the relaxed state and the confidence needed to guide my intuition. I tried to see the world as Peter would. I saw in my mind the skyscrapers of Manhattan turn into a mountain range, and the clouds transform themselves into stars, Peter Max-type stars. And this is what I drew.

It turned out to be an exact replica of what Peter drew. Later Peter would say in an interview that it wasn't so much that I duplicated the drawing that amazed him, rather that another mind could think like his. That's not some impossible trick. I simply let my imagination fly. Based on my knowledge of Peter Max and the ways in which he sees the things he paints, I was able, in a sense, to become his mind and see through his eyes. It was an exercise in seeing *as he sees*, not in how I thought he would see. With practice, you can do much the same thing with the willing participants around you.

By sharpening our senses and our perceptions as shown, we become better predictors of what's going to happen, and we become better placed to let good things happen to us. Intuition also helps us to understand other people much deeper than their surface behavior. We can feel or sense when another person is deeply troubled or whether or not the person is being honest and truthful.

As in picking up nonverbal cues, the better we know someone the better we are at telling what that person really means as opposed to what they say. That same familiarity facilitates the intuitive process. I have married couples on my shows do thought-sending games, not with me but with each other. One member of the couple looks at a magazine ad (remember, we're trying to keep it random) and tries to project the basic image in the ad to his or her spouse standing a few feet away. Part of the reason this works is that the long-married have all kinds of connections to one another that

---

MIND BUILDER

Take a crack at the following experiment I shot for my TV special. In this particular case, we were filming a married couple, though you can do this with anyone you know well. As the cameras rolled, and per my instructions, the wife put a roll of five-flavor LifeSavers behind her back, snapped it open at random, then popped one in her mouth without looking at it and without showing it to her partner. I encouraged her to taste the LifeSaver, to savor it as fully as if it were the best-tasting thing on earth, and then to project that intense taste across the room to her husband.

Her husband, meanwhile, was told to try to taste the LifeSaver in his own mouth, to imagine the flavor his wife tasted. He thought about it for a minute and finally said "Cherry."

It was cherry.

PLAY IT AGAIN, MIND BUILDER

The next time you phone someone or they call you, close your eyes and imagine the color of the shirt they're wearing. Do this often, and you'll wind up getting it right more often than not. Why does this work? I have no idea.

You can use a deck of playing cards to develop your intuitive side, to the point where you rely on it automatically. This exercise involves a regular 52-card deck and tests your intuitive powers. Some might call what we're about to do clairvoyance, which is a French word that means "clear-seeing." That's an apt label, since the game involves sensing something there is no ordinary way you could know.

Take a deck of cards and mix them thoroughly, keeping them face down. Take the top card (face down) and try to sense if it's a black card or a red one. Try to picture or feel the color. If you think it's red, place it in a separate pile on your left, face down. Take the next card and try to sense the color. If you feel it's black, place it in a separate pile on your right, face down. Continue this procedure until you've gone through the entire deck. You can go as fast or as slowly as you wish. The important thing is to go with your first gut feeling. Don't change your mind.

Once you've sorted through the entire 52 cards, turn the two piles over. Count how many red cards are in the pile you thought was red. Count how many black cards are in the pile you thought was black. If you have 12 to 14 correct cards in each pile, that's average; 15 to 20 is excellent; more than 20 is extraordinary.

allow them to pick up cues from their spouses. I always love the looks on people's faces when one says, "Oreos?" and the other turns around a picture of an Oreo cookie. Though they are always astonished, their success is easy to explain: They can jump right into games like this because they already know each other well.

As we've seen, people who've been together for years have a communication link that mirrors the kinds of things I talk about in this book. Though they haven't consciously tried to achieve that, the longer a couple stays together, the more they pick up each other's thoughts. A wife knows, sometimes, when the phone rings that her husband has news for her. A husband can finish his wife's sentences (annoying though that may be). It is the emotional connection shared by those two people that facilitates communication. That and long patience and practice.

With the right mind tools, you can shortcut this process and achieve rapport with people you barely know. Similarly, just as we know our intimates better than we think we do, so do we all possess knowledge we don't realize we have. By tapping into the secrets in your mind, you can tap into the personal power that will enable you to make the most of your life and the most of your world.

MENTAL SOLUTIONS

You've now developed a host of mental abilities to help you solve your problems. Here are a few additional ways to apply those tools and help you to find the answers inside. Remember, these mental exercises exist to strengthen your mind and make your perceptions sharper. Use them! They will empower you.

Start by concentrating 100 percent on the problem, question, or goal at hand to engage your inner mind. Really work at it, like a puppy with a bone. Completely immerse yourself. You'll even want to jot it down on paper, in as few words as you can so you can get to the essence or core of the issue. This alone will help prompt the solution.

Ironically, letting go and doing something completely different—like going to a movie, taking a walk, cleaning the house, or simply meditating—can also trigger solutions.

Or you can do both of the above. Sound contradictory? It's not.

First you worry the problem to death, then you let it go, thereby giving both your conscious and your unconscious minds a whack at it.

Remember the relaxation techniques back when? In addition to helping you achieve success with any of the mind tools provided in this program, they can be used as a conduit for many things, including answering questions that are troubling you.

Sit down, relax, and take a few deep breaths.

Ask yourself the question you want answered. The question must be as specific as possible. Questions such as "Why am I not rich?" "Who will I marry?" "Will I win the lottery?" "Will I get promoted?" not only aren't under your direct control but they are too general and susceptible to outside influences. The more specific and precise the question, the clearer and speedier the answer.

"What is the one thing more than anything else that is blocking money from flowing into my life?"

"Where do I need to go to attract my ideal mate?"

"What is blocking my career at the moment?"

"What is the one thing I should be doing to attract the attention of my superiors that will rocket me upward in my work and career?"

These are the kinds of questions you need to ask.

Now focus on an object in the room that appeals to you—maybe a flower, a picture, a clock. As you concentrate on it, allow the image it forms in your mind to change. It may blur, go all fuzzy, change shape, or transform into different images. Record or make mental notes of everything—items, shapes, colors, smells, sensations, and feelings—that comes to your mind.

Done? My bet is that you've now got the solution you were seeking. By focusing on something external, you free up the answer inside you. Focusing on an object is the means to an end. It's almost as though the monotony allows you to focus and then break through. Sometimes there are multiple answers, and that in itself is a revelation. The point is the answers are there, they're just sometimes way down deep inside of us. You have to get at them.

Meditation and breathing—the basic elements of the total relaxation mindscript—may also help, along with exercise and prayer. Though they sound a bit more new age-y, many people also rely on *chanting* and *contemplation* to tap into their innermost selves. Chanting is the singing of a short, simple melody or even a few monotonous notes that often involves repetition of the same words or sounds in order to attain a spiritual state. Contemplation involves deep thought or reflection as a type of meditation or prayer. You focus your thought on a single concept—NFL, for example—as a way of reaching a more spiritual state. These are all the same paths to the mountaintop. Use as many as work for you, and use them often.

INTUITION MINDSCRIPTS

To tap deeper into your intuition, you need to practice listening to your inner self. These mindscripts will help you accomplish that. Let's say you have met someone and are not sure how you feel about him or her. Use the following "animal" technique to tap into your intuitive feelings about a personal or business relationship, whether new or old.

You Animal, You

Sit comfortably, relax, take a few deep breaths, and picture the person you want to know more about. See them in your mind's eye. Allow the person to turn into an animal. What attributes does this animal suggest to you? A tiger might be menacing and attacking, or strong, gentle, and protective. Is it young or old? Notice all its characteristics. Does any part of it become more prominent or particularly attract your attention? See the animal moving. Where is it going and what is it doing? What qualities suggest themselves to you? When you open your eyes, analyze what this means to you.

A tennis player tried this technique on herself. She thought she would see herself as a tiger on the court, strong and methodical, fierce and competitive. Instead, the animal that came to mind was a gazelle, swift and light-footed, which she realized upon reflection was, in her case, more accurate. She had thought that her principal asset on the court was her fierce, win-at-all-costs competitive spirit (the tiger), but she figured out that it was in fact her speed and grace that were powering her across the court.

Think of Mohammed Ali's "float like a butterfly, sting like a bee" line. He carefully chose the exact animals to convey his lightness of foot and his ruthless method of attack. A bee, after all, is willing to die to defeat his attacker. It is impossible to imagine a different set of animals representing Ali.

I worked closely with New York Giants' Jason Sehorn and Michael Strahan. Both used this technique, visualizing, among other things, the radar sense of a bat. They were able to pick up the slightest movement of the opposition, and thus knew what to avoid and what to head toward. They went all the way to the Super Bowl that year. And I am firmly convinced that they got there partly through these "batty" visualization techniques. Every animal has a power; it is up to you to decide what that power means to you and how you will use it.

You can also use this animal technique to answer a question. Close your eyes, ask the question to yourself a few times, and then allow the animal image to form. Continue as above, asking yourself the questions to interpret the answer.

Here's another way to go.

Paint Yourself into the Picture

Let your body relax as previously explained, and visualize a scene from nature that has great personal appeal for you. Perhaps you are surveying a magnificent view from a mountaintop. Or maybe you're in a field, beside a lake, or by the sea. Your location of choice may be somewhere that has strong memories for you or somewhere you would like to visit. If you are having difficulty visualizing such a scene, choose a painting you particularly like, one that depicts a quiet, calm, and relaxing view of nature, and use that. See yourself in this scene, surrounded by and at one with the forces of nature.

Be aware of everything around you. Soak it all in. Picture all the colors, the different hues. Appreciate the shapes of the trees, the plants, the animals. Notice the clouds taking shape and moving, the water flowing. Hear all the sounds, no matter how small—if any are indistinct, focus in on them. As you breathe, smell the aromas, the fragrances. Breathe them in and savor them. Feel the movement around you, the breeze, the flight of the birds, the animals you can see and the ones you can't. Feel the movement in the earth beneath you. Feel the movement of the water and the life it contains. Drink the water, taste the fruit of the trees, the nectar from the flowers, be totally at peace with the scene you are a part of.

Breathe in and out, concentrating on its rhythm. In this state, allow your intuition to reveal itself to you. Do not go looking for answers; permit the answers to come to you. Whatever thoughts float through your mind, describe them aloud. If possible, use a tape recorder. Otherwise a friend with pen and paper could help. You can change places later and you can record your friend's thoughts. If you cannot record them as you speak, write them down immediately after you have finished.

Describe your feelings, what you see, hear, touch, taste, and smell—everything, no matter how trivial. Whatever thoughts and pictures come into your mind, try to remember them or put them in your PDA. Later you will come to interpreting these thoughts. Do not fight the direction you are going. Allow yourself to be led.

You will be amazed at what will be revealed to you. I promise.

One note: There is nothing like solitude for getting in touch with your inner self. Outside, take a walk up the mountains, through the woods, or along the beach on your own. At home, close the doors and switch off the phones and any other external interruptions. You may choose to do nothing or just to contemplate. The main thing is you have time on your own. Performing one of the above intuitive exercises after a period of solitude will prove extremely beneficial.

DIGGING DEEPER

We're all involved in this intuitive dance. We can either learn the steps and dance with grace and power, or we can step on other people's toes and get tromped on in turn. But this is the dance of life: The one thing we can't afford to do is sit this one out and become wallflowers. So if we're going to stomp this metaphor into the proverbial ground, put on your dancing shoes and let's learn the next step in your dance repertoire.

How do you develop your intuitive nature? For starters, by seeing coincidences as more than circumstantial and following them up.

You've applied for a job in a company where you really want to work and a junior high-school friend calls and tells you she was recently hired there.

You've just decided to go on a trip to Italy when your best friend calls and says that they too are planning a trip to Italy.

You go to that obscure restaurant that you've never been to before and run into someone you had been meaning to call.

You have a dream about a favorite uncle. In the morning you receive a call to tell you he died the previous evening.

You pick up the phone to call your buddy and discover he's already on the line—having called you at the same time.

Many people brush these experiences aside as mere coincidences, but there's nothing mere about them. They are all examples of synchronicity. Whether we know it or not, they happen for a reason. And we can be more attuned to make them happen and be prepared when they do.

To fully use this sixth sense, you need to become more self-aware. You can do so by paying close attention to your inner dialogue, the voice inside your head that murmurs messages about your life and your self-image. Often when I speak with students, I pick up on how much they put themselves down or engage in what is often called *negative self-talk*. This type of thinking drowns out what your intuition may be trying to whisper in your ear. It also defeats your efforts at trying to create positive change.

Creating a concrete image of what you want to achieve works in various ways. Visualization sends a signal to your intuitive side about what you want. Then your intuition can begin to put the moves in motion that will make your desires become real. But don't expect your intuition to do it all alone. That's where the second part, taking action, comes in.

Your tasks are to focus on your goals and then act on your intuitive impulses. Pay attention to any clue from your intuition that may help you achieve your goal. You may have a sudden impulse to call a friend. Call! You might feel drawn to read a certain book. Read it! You may have a sudden impulse to speak to the person standing next to you in line. Talk!

Action and intuition work off each other to accomplish your goal. Your intuitive "higher mind" can see the overview of what it needs to do to pull all the events together and help you accomplish what you want. Have confidence that your inner voice isn't leading you astray. To the contrary.

We all have access to our intuitive and creative abilities, which are infinite. We are not all fighting for a share of a limited pie. You can breathe in all the air you like. It will not affect anyone else. There is more than enough for everyone. The oxygen in the air is constantly replenished by the plant life every day. Likewise you cannot deplete the abundant creativity in the universe. Use it. It is always there, as is your intuition.

Even obvious, logical decisions should be referred to the intuition to see if they feel right. Hold up a decision to your intuition and say, "Is this a good one?" Your answer to yourself should be clear; if it's not, that's a message, too. Intuition works best when used with your thinking mind. They complement each other, especially now that your newly trained thinking mind is first-rate, and the resultant whole is greater than the sum of the parts. Do not skip the logical exploration of the question.

A caveat: If you fear what your intuition might reveal, then your intuition will not be free to reveal itself to you. You may need professional counseling to release those demons. Your intuitive mind is there to help and guide you, not to put obstacles in your way. It is also difficult sometimes to interpret what your intuition is showing you. The temptation is to see what you want instead of what is revealed. You have to practice being open to what you are telling yourself in order to have any success with your intuition.

STOKING YOUR INTUITION

To take full advantage of your intuitive facilities, you must act on the intuitive answers you get. If you do not follow through, your inner mind will not take you seriously. Suppose a friend contacts you. He has an urgent problem. A research reference is needed and he can't locate it anywhere. Can you help? With your connections you track one down. It takes you several days. You could have been doing other things, but you want to help your friend. You bring the book to his house. You call back a week later. The book is on the table, still shrink-wrapped. He hasn't even looked at it. How would

MIND BUILDER

Mindgame cards

You are developing all the pieces you'll need in your mental toolbox to put the whole puzzle together and make it work for you. There are five designs in our Mindgame pack. A full pack consists of 25 cards, five each of each design. Simply photocopy them on heavy stock and cut them out.

There are two main types of experiment for which the Mindgame pack can be used: (1) pick up cues from the cards or (2) pick up cues from another person.

In picking up cues from the cards, the cards are shuffled and you try to guess each card before it is put aside. Keep a running list. Then count the hits and misses.

For picking up cues from another person, a friend picks a card and thinks of it. You then try to ascertain the design. Since the experimenter

you feel? Used? Supposing he made a similar request every week for a few weeks, and you helped out again and still your friend didn't act on what you did for him. Pretty soon you would be fed up with this and wouldn't bother. You would switch off, wouldn't you?

Your subconscious responds the same way. Use the information it provides and next time it will be like a small child, eager to help. Once it sees that you are serious, it will start to produce brilliant (though occasionally less than practical) solutions to your problems. If it gives you an idea for a pressing problem, act on it straight knows the nature of the card, you may be picking out subconscious clues that are being inadvertently sent.

Scientists believe that you have a 20 to 25 percent chance of guessing the correct answer. So if you have five cards, you should, on average, be able to guess one correctly. Any percentages over 25 percent would mean you may have a high intuitive ability.

Calculate the percentage of correct answers and graph your hits and misses. Remember, the more times you run the experiment, the more convincing your evidence becomes (each time you go through the 25 cards, it's called a run). If your hit-to-miss ratio improves over time, that means you're strengthening your intuitive abilities.

	Correct	Incorrect
1st		
2nd		
3rd		
4th		
5th		
6th		
7th		

away if at all feasible. Some ideas, no matter how brilliant, won't be usable, at least not immediately. Even so, write all these down in your journal. By acknowledging the subconscious in this way, you let it know you appreciate the ideas and encourage it to keep working for you.

Speaking of appreciation, don't forget to thank your subconscious for its efforts. I know it sounds daft, thanking yourself, but your subconscious thrives on appreciation. You don't have to buy a bouquet of flowers and a box of chocolates or the new Dylan CD

MIND BUILDER

Go to a neighborhood you've never been to before and wander. Better yet, get lost. You don't have to look lost (i.e., vulnerable), just open your mind to what's there. Then try to make your way home.

---

for it, but you do have to acknowledge to yourself that your subconscious has helped you out. Feeling good, solving a problem—those are the rewards for listening to your intuition. Acknowledge that!

TRY THIS

THE SALEM INTUITION TEST (S.I.T.)

Here is a questionnaire that will help you assess your basic style of approaching problems and decisions. To the degree that there is a correlation between intuitive style and the quality of intuition, your score might show how good your intuitive abilities are as well. For each item, choose the answer that BEST applies to you.

1. In school or work I usually agree with my managers/teachers:
   A. yes
   B. no

2. When reading books, I usually enjoy:
   A. fiction
   B. true stories
   C. about equal

3. Basically I see things:
   A. as they are
   B. as I think they ought to be

4. When my intuition differs from the facts, I usually:
   A. trust the facts
   B. listen to my feelings

5. I prefer multitasking:
   A. yes
   B. no

6. When I don't see eye to eye with others, I:
   A. let them know about it
   B. keep it to myself

7. Broadly:
   A. I am a risk taker
   B. I play it safe

8. I tend to get deja vu:
   A. seldom
   B. often
   C. never

9. Logic is overrated as a virtue:
   A. true
   B. false

10. When faced with new situations, I:
   A. am excited
   B. am uncomfortable

11. Do you remember your dreams?

    A. yes

    B. no

12. Have you ever had a dialogue with a nonexistent or a dead person (as a talk, not as a medium)?

    A. yes

    B. no

13. I embrace uncertainty:

    A. yes

    B. no

14. How many fingers am I holding up now as I type:

    A. none

    B. one

    C. two

    D. three or more

15. I tend to:

    A. live in the moment

    B. fret often about the future

    C. look regularly at the triumphs of my past

16. When learning something new, I:

    A. meticulously study the manual

    B. get started and learn the rules as I go along

17. At work I am thought of as:

    A. a pragmatic individual

    B. a visionary

18. Multiple choice tests do not give me a chance to express myself:
>   A. true
>   B. false

19. How many people are born on this planet each day?
>   A. fewer than 190,000
>   B. more than 190,000

20. Most of the people I hang out with:
>   A. believe in intuition
>   B. are skeptical

21. I have many experiences and ideas that I can't explain:
>   A. true
>   B. false
>   C. not many

22. In reading data, I prefer:
>   A. graphs
>   B. statistics
>   C. anecdotes

23. I can usually be convinced by an appeal:
>   A. to reason
>   B. to my emotions

24. I think that puns are:
>   A. the highest form of humor
>   B. the lowest form of humor
>   C. undecided

25. Have you ever won a lottery where you chose the number?

    A. yes

    B. no

26. Unpredictable people are:

    A. dangerous

    B. interesting

27. I am best known as a detail person:

    A. true

    B. false

28. When my plans are stymied, I:

    A. freak out

    B. make a new plan

29. I follow my hunches:

    A. regularly

    B. almost never

Scoring

Give yourself one point if you answered "A" on the following items: 2, 5, 6, 7, 9, 10, 11, 12, 13, 15, 18, 20, 21, 24, 25

Give yourself one point if you answered "B" on the following items: 1, 3, 4, 8, 16, 17, 19, 23, 26, 27, 28

Give yourself one point if you answered "C" on the following items: 14, 22, 24

If your total score is 23 or above, you tend strongly toward an intuitive approach to decisions and problems. More than

likely you trust your intuition, as well you should, since it it
probably highly accurate!

If your total is between 15 and 22, you tend to vary in style
but are more intuitive than analytic or systematic. Your
intuition is probably correct more often than not.

If your total is between 8 and 14, you tend to mix styles but
lean more toward the analytic and rational than the intuitive.
Your intuition might be a bit uncertain.

If you total is below 8, you lean heavily toward a systematic,
rational approach to problems and decisions. Chances are
you do not trust your intuition very much, perhaps due to
past experiences when it has been wrong.

Do not regard this test as a definitive measure of your intuitive
capacity. A high score on the questionnaire is merely a good indica-
tion of positive, intuition-enhancing behavior. The questions, therefore, can also serve as a tool for introspection and improvement.

CHAPTER 7

MIND AND MEMORY (KEY 5)

CONCENTRATION

During my stage performance, I often always ask the hugest audience member I can find to come up onstage and try to push me over. You should have seen the size of the guy when I did this same act at the London Correctional Facility in London, Ohio. He looked like a cross between Shaquille O'Neal and the Incredible Hulk. I came up to his third prison-blue uniform shirt button and could have wrapped that shirt around me twice over. Undaunted, I closed my eyes and visualized myself as a pillar of rock, immoveable. I nodded to signal that I was ready. The Hulk put his hands on my shoulders, spread his feet apart for leverage, and put his huge weight behind a big push. You could see his muscles bulge with the effort. To his consternation—and the delighted guffaws of his fellow prisoners—this giant of a man was not able to budge me, an admittedly nonathletic little guy. Just a case of mind over muscle. You are now ready to break out of the mental box you've built around your brain while increasing your mental capacity and maintaining mental agility. Engaging and improving your memory will increase your ability to visualize, create, and think. In addition, the better you are at concentrating and remembering, the more readily you will be able to pick up the cues in Part 1 and put them together and take advantage of the information they provide.

MIND BUILDER

For most of us, the mind-body connection is little more than an overused phrase—until we try it out for ourselves. You have greater influence than you know. Try the following exercise and see how your thoughts can affect your body:

Extend both your arms straight out in front of you. Turn your left palm face up to the ceiling. Your right palm is face down to the floor. Close your eyes. You didn't close your eyes, did you? You kept reading. Good. Continue reading so you know what it is you're supposed to be doing here. Got it? THEN close your eyes.

Begin concentrating on your left arm. Imagine it's holding a bucket of bricks and it's getting heavier and heavier. And every few seconds someone is dropping another brick into the bucket.

At the same time, imagine that a string is tied to your right wrist. That string goes upward and is tied to a large helium balloon. Your right arm is getting lighter and lighter; the balloon is dragging it up, up, up into the air.

Continue to alternate these thoughts. Left arm feeling so very heavy, right arm getting lighter and lighter. Keep these thoughts going for 1 to 2 minutes. At the same time, you should be keeping both arms straight in front of you, level with one another. Open your eyes. The difference in the positions of your arms should be very apparent.

If you are doing this in a group, have everyone stretch out their arms and close their eyes. Simply tell them out loud to imagine the lightness and heaviness. Keep up a running stream of instructions for a minute or two and then have them open their eyes.

Want more proof? Hold both of your hands in front of you. Now, imagine the blood flow is increasing in one hand. Visualize it as clearly as possible. Keep this up for about a minute. Now ask a friend which hand looks redder. It will be the hand you were visualizing.

Finally, engaging your mind in challenges can increase not only your mental abilities but also perhaps even stave off the onset of dementia. Indeed, sophisticated cognitive activity may build neural connections that thwart Alzheimer's. Brain cells, or neurons, may shrink as we age. But neurons don't just die off by the thousands starting shortly after birth, as scientists once believed. We now know that the brain exhibits plasticity, allowing neural connections to be forged even late in life. Novel activities may actually "cross-train" or strengthen neural networks, building agility and disease resistance. A study published in 2002 in the *Journal of the American Medical Association* found that people who regularly read, solve crossword puzzles, play cards, do puzzles, work out riddles, and practice other mental stimulation may prevent dementia of all types.

Since ancient times, man has been curious about the manner in which the mind and body coexist. While many have put forward the idea that they operate separately, more recent thought and research on the subject have spawned the belief that they work in unison. This has triggered the development of holistic approaches to medicine, environment, and pleasure, in which the human being is viewed as an integrated "whole."

Many examples of the close relationship between body and mind can be seen in our everyday lives. The effect that physical processes can have on the mind is clear, for instance, when coffee with caffeine is consumed. Caffeine is a stimulant of the central nervous system and thereby increases levels of concentration and alertness. Excessive intake of caffeine can lead to physical symptoms, like rapid speech, racing pulse, and anxiety attacks.

Similarly, mental and emotional experiences can be seen to produce definite reactions in the body. For instance, if you become scared or anxious, many things can happen. Your sympathetic nervous system is activated within your body, resulting in a release of adrenaline from your adrenal glands into your bloodstream and a quickening of your respiration and heart rate. Blood flow is diverted from areas such as the bowel and skin to tissue such as muscle, heart, and lung. The net effect is to prepare you to take "action" and be "alert." On the other hand, if you are thinking pleasant thoughts and feeling calm, your body will be more relaxed, with your breathing slow and even and your heart beating at a normal pace.

We've explored how to see, hear, and even decipher the hidden and nonverbal cues around us that we've spent a lifetime ignoring. As you're about to see, however, unlocking your mind power isn't just a matter of focusing, though that's an important step. You have to concentrate, not just in one but in two ways in order to fully benefit from your mental capabilities.

NOW CONCENTRATE

Even the simplest experience requires that you impose order on a series of disconnected elements. You both *concentrate* the experience—organizing it based on rules and biology, and distilling it to its basics the same way a cook concentrates the flavors in a sauce by boiling off the liquid—and *concentrate on* the experience by focusing on it to the exclusion of other input.

Let's start at the beginning (always a good idea) and look at how our brains organize experience, either consciously or unconsciously.

In our conscious minds we set up an underlying structure on which we can drape our experiences. It's a comfort thing. We are comfortable with the structure we create, and we want the world to conform to that structure. Americans, for example, tend to organize their time into "work" and "play." These notions are part of that structure. Too bad they're almost entirely arbitrary. Part of what I'm trying to do here is to get you to recognize the conscious structure you have set up and maybe, just maybe, rethink some of that structure and let it build itself in different ways.

When you unconsciously organize experience, you follow certain rules to pull together the perceptions in your mind. The goblet twin figure is a famous example. You perceive white and black shapes, but you concentrate it—that is, you organize it—into a picture by putting some of the shapes in the background and some in the foreground. What is figure and what is background will constantly shift. The same holds true for all of your reality around you. What you focus on and what is background are conditions based on a wide range of factors. Is the bottle on the table or is the table under the bottle?

What is background, what is foreground—the choice is yours.

You usually concentrate or organize experience by giving priority to what is striking or outstanding. By concentrating on the less dominant or background image, however, you wind up seeing a completely different picture.

Don't beat yourself up about it, though. We do this in all situations. We never experience everything about anything. Instead, we connect the dots, so to speak, to allow ourselves to make meaning out of that experience. By helping ourselves to consider more than our knee-jerk, dot-connecting tendencies, we can expand not only our thought processes but also how we actually experience the world around us. Connect all the dots by using only *four straight lines* and without raising your pencil from the paper once you begin. Force yourself to think outside the box. You can find the solution on page 223.

•   •   •

•   •   •

•   •   •

As you see, the solution is only possible if you LITERALLY think outside the box.

So why am I bothering you with this? Think about a brand-new pair of Levi's. Remember when Levi's all used to come shrink-to-fit? Those are the kind of jeans I'm talking about. They were stiff, and dark, and hard to wear. But as you wore them and washed them and wore them again, they became uniquely yours, fitting you (and no one else) like no other pair of jeans. Your experiences are like that: They make things fit on your structure. By opening yourself up, you see more and experience more, which in turn enriches the experiences themselves and makes them *fit* you.

Without a doubt, concentration is a vital factor in developing the mind's ability to control itself. True concentration, in its fullest sense, consists of focusing the mind on an idea, or totally fixing attention on a physical object. By doing this you can eliminate outside distractions.

CONCENTRATION MINDSCRIPT

Here is an exercise to help retool your mind and increase its ability to concentrate. I call it time watching:

For the best results, use a watch with a large second hand that sweeps around the dial, although one with a smaller second hand will do.

- Place the watch where you can study it closely. Set the hour and minute hands at exactly 12 o'clock so that they will not interfere with your watching the second hand move around the dial.

- Wait until the second hand has reached the 12 o'clock position; then, as a preliminary test, let your eyes follow its trip around the dial until you tire or lose interest. Note how many seconds it took for that to happen.

- Take a brief rest, then repeat the experiment, trying to carry it further. You will probably find it almost impossible to keep your thoughts from wandering during the brief time span of a single minute.

- Keep repeating this as a regular exercise and you will note steady improvement. Be sure to take sufficient rest periods. You are not out to set an endurance record but to develop your powers of concentration.

- Continue this until you find you can reach the minute mark without distraction. By focusing on the seconds themselves, by counting them off mentally, you will help ensure attention.

- Continue the exercise; increase up to 2 minutes, or longer if you wish.

Repeating this exercise periodically will help you develop the ability to tap that level of concentration when you need it.

"AH YES, I REMEMBER IT WELL"

Memory is a powerful facet of the way your mind works and the ways in which you perceive the world around you. It is part of that catalog of experience that we organize out of everyday reality. Without it, all concentrating comes to nothing.

A good memory and an active mind feed each other. Amazingly, though most of us fear the loss of our memories even more than death, we rarely do what it takes to conserve or strengthen them. As you're about to see, that's just not a tough thing to do.

We do not have to buy into the notion that memory inevitably fades with age. The German poet Goethe wrote well into his 80s. George Abbott, a name long known on Broadway, remained involved with the theater into his late 90s. George Burns reached 100, Picasso produced works in his 90s, and some of George Bernard Shaw's best-known works were written after he passed the 70 mark. Even the Rolling Stones seem pretty much on top of things in their mid-60s. An active mind indicates a good memory, regardless of age.

Our brain is a more complex mechanism than the most sophisticated computer. In addition to the mental processes, its primary functions are thought, memory, and imagination. It consists of some 10 billion interconnected nerve cells with innumerable extensions—by far the most incredible bit of miniaturization known to man, far superior to the revolutionary chip containing circuitry responsible for the operation of the computers that govern the way we live today.

Despite the wonders of science, technology, and medical and psychological research, memory still remains an unsolved challenge to the scientist. Neuroscientists, psychologists, and biologists have yet to agree on how we remember. Biologists and psychologists theorize that memories are the result of electrical and chemical impulses our brain receives when it is exposed to stimuli taken in by our five senses. What we see, hear, smell, touch, and taste stimulates our cells to fire off signals to our brain.

Although scientists are experimenting with drugs and chemicals, it may still be years before researchers can understand how pharmaceuticals, now in the experimental stages, can improve our memory. The laboratory "memory pill" has yet to be discovered.

Psychologists, however, confirm what every memory expert knows—the best way to remember is to weave new information into the mind through the use of mnemonics (named for the Greek goddess of memory, Mnemosyne). To put it another way, the science or art of improving memory involves the use of certain formulas or other aids to help us in remembering.

These tricks of the mind work because they allow you to fit hard-to-remember facts into a context that already exists in your mind. We improve memory by associating easily forgotten routine data with earlier remembered sounds or images. It's all part of the dictionary that we make from our experiences. We are refining the filing system in our subconscious so that we can more easily access the data we need to function best in the world.

Here's an easy exercise for starting to train your memory. On the next page is a list of 10 items. Memorize the list to the best of your ability, then see if you can write down all 10 things.

1. Umbrella
2. Telephone
3. Magazine
4. Broom
5. Chewing gum
6. Mouse
7. Hamburger buns
8. Baseball cap
9. Deck of cards
10. Book

Write down your memorized list.

1. _____
2. _____
3. _____
4. _____
5. _____
6. _____
7. _____
8. _____
9. _____
10. _____

Could you do it? I'm guessing it was a stretch, even if you managed, and more likely that you couldn't. Here's a way not only to remember those items but also to remember them in order.

Picture yourself holding an umbrella and talking on a phone. A magazine blows past your feet, followed by an earnest, broom-wielding, gum-chewing mouse. The mouse is busily sweeping and chewing when suddenly, he is trapped in the grip of a hamburger bun. Mouseburgers! On the bun is a full-color picture of a baseball cap (you supply the team colors—just be sure to take the trouble to imagine it fully). Trapped though he is, the mouse suggests a quick game of cards. He deals a hand from the deck he has pulled out of the bun. You do not dignify his presence with a reply. Instead, you pull out a book and begin to read.

Now, read this script more than once and take the time to really see the story happening, like a little movie in your head. Then write down the 10 objects.

Write down your memorized list.

1._____

2._____

3._____

4._____

5._____

6._____

7._____

8._____

9._____

10._____

I'll wager you did a whole lot better the second time around.

Whether or not we are conscious of it, we have all used mnemonic devices, or memory tricks, from the time we were children. We made associations. We remembered the musical notes on the staff by the sentence Every Good Boy Does Fine—the initials translate to the notes E, G, B, D, and F. As schoolchildren, we recited, "In fourteen hundred and ninety-two, Columbus sailed the ocean blue," to remember the date of his discovery. Even today, most of us remember to turn our clocks forward in spring and back in fall with the help of the phrase, "Spring forward, Fall back."

A most common mnemonic device is the acronym—we know

that NFL stands for the National Football League; IBM, International Business Machines; FBI, the Federal Bureau of Investigation, and NASCAR . . . well, well . . . you know. You can create your own acronyms for things you need to remember. Just keep in mind that your personal acronyms won't be understood by anyone else! Families often develop this kind of shorthand so that children can be admonished in front of company without being embarrassed. My Hebrew name, Moshe, is a great device for remembering the five Great Lakes—Michigan, Ontario, Superior, Huron, and Erie.

There is no limit to what you can imagine. And when you tie that limitless quality to the process of consciously remembering things, you've got a potent system of memory management.

WHAT'S IN A NAME?

When was the last time you said, "I can place the face, but I can't remember the name"? Recently would be my bet. When we are introduced to someone, we usually forget their name while we are shaking hands! Yet names are the most powerful words we have in working with people. To be able to call an associate at a business meeting by name when everybody else is merely staring blankly at them is a potent advancer for you in the world of business. Our names are who we are. To not call somebody by name is to be dismissive of that person. In short, remembering a person's name is a way to foster a relationship. Or, as I said earlier, it is magic.

Unfortunately, this critical memory test is the very one that so many of us fail. One college professor who was unable to remember the names of the students in his classes came to me for help.

"Look, you already know the name of the biggest troublemaker in each class and the smart guy in each class, don't you?" I asked him.

He replied in the affirmative, as I knew he would. Since I knew he would reprimand whoever that troublemaker was all the time, and call on the smart guy, the repetition would have cemented those names in his mind. Everybody knows the name of the biggest troublemaker; it's inevitable. "Bob, stop it." "Bob, go to the office." "Bob, put down that chicken."

For the less noticeable students in the class, I advised him to make a list of their names and jot down memory cues about each. The first time he called on a student by name, I suggested that he find out a little about them, and then make some connection between their name, their physical appearance, and their identity. It's called association.

Let's say he has a student whose name is DJ Saliman. The student stands up and right away it's obvious that he's from India and very tall. That helps. So the professor thinks "DJ," and visualizes this tall guy playing records in India, surrounded by saris hung up on the wall. So now he has his first name. He still needs to find an association for the last name Saliman. Maybe he sees DJ in a sailboat. So he remembers DJ Sailing Man, which gives him the basic structure of the name. He may also have tried seeing a disc jockey (DJ) spinning a salmon on a turntable. Many routes are only limited by your imagination.

In addition to helping the professor remember better, making these connections helped him be more creative as well. And that made him a better teacher. One thing leads to another and another. It's not just one element. I didn't just give him the power of memory. I gave him the power of visualization and the power of working with intuitions. By building his feelings about the kids he was teaching into his name creation bag, the professor was able to exercise his intuitive perceptions. Later he might find out that he was right, or he might find out that he was wrong. Maybe the student hates sailing. Well, now that the professor has learned that DJ hates water, he can remember the name even better when he thinks Sailor Man. Perhaps that dread of water was what prompted him to come up with that particular memory cue.

If you have trouble remembering names, you can take solace in the fact that you're far from alone. Because most of us are visually oriented, we see the person to whom we are introduced far longer than we hear the name. We may be with the party for an entire evening, and the face is indelibly printed in our memory. But we hear the name for a fraction of a second, and during that short time most of us are thinking of something else (nice tie he's wearing; I wonder where I've seen her before; oh, there's Jim over there; what will I say once introductions are over?). So the name makes no impression. To remember a name you must hear it, concentrate on it, repeat it, and repeat it again. Say the person's name at meeting and at parting, and drop the name into the conversation wherever you think it will lend weight to what you are saying or whenever you can find a plausible excuse. You are introduced to Mr. Fischer. Say, "I'm happy to meet you, Mr. Fischer. How do you spell your name . . . sh or sch?" Mr. Fischer senses an interest in him, enough interest to want to have him spell his name. When you part, repeat again, "It was nice meeting you, Mr. Fischer." You have used the name twice, and having repeated it, you have made an impression in your mind. You concentrated.

Next, make an association with the name. The name Fischer calls to mind immediately a man fishing, a piece of fishing tackle, a hook, bait, lure, or whatever comes first to your mind. Form a mental picture of the name. Every name can be imagined in some form of a substitute word. There are names that have meaning, that suggest, that are visual, that are famous, and foreign names that conjure up a picture instantly. Here are but a few:

Names with Meaning	Names That Suggest	Visual Names	Famous Names	Foreign Names
Carpenter	Welch	Bear	Kennedy	Schneider
Mason	Kellogg	Fox	Burton	Kashuwa
Fisher	Campbell	Robbins	Marx	Applebaum
Smith	Heinz	Hawk	Grant	Linowitz
Miller	Gillette	Polo	Letterman	Jimenez
Taylor	McDonald	Ford	Franklin	Pappagallo
Baker	Krystal	Hart	Glenn	Lovenheim
Shuster	Denny	Lemmon	Martin	Pandolfini
Farmer	Remington	Wolf	Rothschild	Weiskopf

With practice you will quickly be able to form a visual identification. Mr. Weissman may suggest an owl; Mrs. Keebler a cracker; Mr. Berger a hamburger.

The meaningful words you have substituted do not have to be exact; a sound-alike will still help the name to be recalled. Try to keep the first syllable or part of the name unchanged, if possible.

Here are a few more examples to get you going:

- Linowitz—a line of witches

- Sutton—a 1960s-style sit-in

- Pappagallo—Papa wearing a 10-gallon hat

- Elvebakk—the back of Santa's elves

Finally, make a rapid association with a facial or physical characteristic and associate the substitute words with an outstanding physical characteristic. See the line of witches on Mr. Linowitz's long nose, or a bunch of radical protesters entangled in Ms. Sutton's hair. The more outrageous the easier it will be to remember . . . and only you will know.

MAKE IT EASY ON YOURSELF

Just as there are different learning styles, there are different memory styles. We both learn and remember by listening, by seeing, and by doing. Emotional experiences and stressful events have a particular tendency to imprint permanent associations in our memory file. Asked where you were on August 9, 1995, you might not have the slightest recollection. But mention September 11, 2001, and you no doubt know exactly where you were at the time you learned of the terror attacks. If you are old enough, you'll remember exactly where you were and what you were doing on November 22, 1963, when you learned of the Kennedy assassination. These constitute associations that you will never forget.

Incidents, facts, or details that don't pack an emotional punch are harder to remember. By recognizing your particular style, you can enhance your memory, for just as there are different thinking styles (as we learned last week), there are different ways to remember.

People who remember best what they hear we call "ear minded." The ear-minded person profits most from lectures, from what he hears.

Those who remember best what they see are referred to as "eye minded." The eye-minded person will remember exactly where on a page he saw a certain ad, or an article, and when scanning the magazine or paper looks only in that location. He will best remember what he sees.

To determine whether you're predominantly eye- or ear-minded, read a paragraph in a book, close the book, and recall as many details as you can remember from the reading. Then have a friend read an equivalent paragraph out loud, and recall what you have heard. The results will help identify your memory tendencies.

Some people remember best things related to a particular motion. These are classified as "motor minded." A predominantly motor-minded person relies on his other senses: touch, smell, and taste.

While most people tend toward one of these three categories, we all employ each one of these various memory faculties to a greater or lesser degree when learning and remembering. No one is 100 percent eye, ear, or motor minded. Still, it is important to recognize our mental biases. How do we learn and find out things best? Are we visual people? Are we aural people? Do we work best when physical movement is involved?

To keep trying to put a square peg in a round hole makes people miserable. Finding out through life experience and through self-analysis what works best for you will quickly make you a lot happier. Are you sharper in the morning or evening? Are you physically dexterous or are you somebody who enjoys reading? Make lists of these traits and figure out where your strengths lie. Then use that list to focus on jobs and situations that suit your personal style. If you're not a morning person, you really shouldn't try to force yourself into a job that requires mental alertness at early hours.

Luckily, you can also rely on external aids no matter what your personal memory style. At some point in time, we have all experienced a mental blank. You're reading a book and suddenly develop a craving for a crisp, cold apple from the refrigerator. You put down the book, walk to the kitchen and when you get there, you have completely forgotten why you went there. You go back to the chair, pick up the book, and instantly remember the reason for the diversion. Your memory returns when you re-create the state you were in originally. Psychologists call this "state dependent recall." For instance, if you are eating chocolate while studying for an exam, eating chocolate while you're taking the exam could help you remember more of what you were studying. (You can thank me later for that one.)

Memory is tied to emotional states as well. Indeed, our memory is woven into all our senses in ways we don't fully understand. We have all had the experience of hearing a familiar piece of music and being able to picture the exact place we first heard it. Those kinds of associations just happen. If you train yourself to make them happen more often, you're a step ahead.

The conscious mind is, however, only part of the process of pumping up our memory—and our minds as a whole. The subconscious constitutes the other major portion of the equation. As we have already discussed, though there are limitations on our senses, that doesn't mean there aren't other things out there. We know that there are colors we can't see, ranges of sounds we can't hear, and a whole host of sensory experiences that we can only touch on the surface. In order to tap into this lot, and the full power of your mind, you have to stimulate your brain, jolt it out of its routines, so it powers up instead of relying on cruise control.

We are creatures of habit. Over time we have developed our set ways of doing things. A quick inventory of your own life will make my point: the way you get up, when you wash, what you have for breakfast, when you leave for the office, and the route you take. At work you will tend to park in the same spot or in the same area of the parking lot. You will either always park face in or you will reverse in.

These habits we've developed form the safety barriers of our comfort zones. They are "at the edge of the envelope" we've created for ourselves. That phrase comes from test pilots testing new models of planes. The first day the pilot will take the plane so high and so fast. That is the current edge of the envelope, or the comfort zone for that plane. Next day, the pilot will go higher and faster, expanding the edge of the envelope. This continues until the plane can travel no higher or faster without serious problems. This is the outer edge of the envelope for that plane.

Very few people make the effort to get out of their comfort zone or to expand their envelope. That's a shame. While there is a limit to how fast and how high any plane can go, I believe that our own mental potential as humans is virtually limitless if we make the effort to stretch our mental boundaries.

Do you have a brain-bending question about how the world works, but no experiment to do or equipment to use that can answer that question? The world's greatest scientists know that creativity is key when it comes to scientific thinking. Some of the most famous theories have popped out of thought experiments— fantastic ways to wonder what the world would be like if things were different. Imagine a world with no gravity. I have no idea what you've imagined, but you've just taken your mind to a place that is totally somewhere else. That's all it takes.

Learn to think beyond your comfort zone. Do you actually see, hear, touch, or even taste amply? What are you missing? To know is to take control of your perceptions. You can, with minimal effort, open back up those fixed, closed ways of looking at your reality by exploring how we all use filters to make sense of "what is out there." By changing our filters and getting out of our own way, we can literally change our reality. This is vital information if we're to understand how we can use our mind in new ways.

So open your mind to new experiences and resources. Learn and re-learn about the world. By opening your mind to experiencing new things or approaching existing routines from a new angle, you are telling your subconscious that it is okay to be open to new ways. Your mind is therefore encouraged to view new experiences positively and, at a deeper level, to be more accepting of that which is not the norm.

This process indirectly opens your own intuitive powers and processes.

In essence, you are training yourself to realize that there is more than one way of achieving a goal. When Thomas Edison invented the lightbulb, he had to make a mental leap in order to find the correct filament that wouldn't just burn up. Most people said it was impossible, that nothing would burn long enough. Most people would have given up. But Edison believed that "invention is 10 percent inspiration and 90 percent perspiration." So he kept on exploring different options and eventually found the key.

After a while your mind will automatically look at problems or decisions from different angles. That habit will prompt you to start perceiving ideas that are unseen by others. Because your mind is no longer conditioned to seeing things "in the comfort zone," it will see the bigger picture.

When renewing learning patterns, do not disregard the obvious. Take time to reflect on your own limitations, expand your goals and development, and seek out continuing education programs. Aim to always learn something new—read books, papers, journals, and make a habit of learning from other people. Just don't let them discourage you, no matter how good their intentions or how seemingly outlandish your ideas. The Wright brothers would never have created the airplane if they hadn't challenged the notion that if God had intended man to fly, he would have given us wings. The world is full of people who say something is impossible and therefore never try it. To say you can't pick up other people's thoughts is to admit defeat before trying.

You can, as I have, take all this even further and train yourself to initiate new experiences. Start by exiting the bed on a different side. It might be the other side of the bed, or the end of the bed. If you dress from the top down, try dressing from the bottom up. If

MIND BUILDER

You may remember one of TV's classic game shows called *Concentration*. With the memory tricks in your mental exercise routine, you would have aced every round and won a bundle. Right? Try this concentration game on for size.

Take a deck of cards and choose 15 pairs of cards. Shuffle this new deck and then arrange the cards in a grid face down on a table in front of you, so that you wind up with five rows of six cards each. Set a timer or check your watch. Now go!

Turn over one card. Turn over another. If they match, pick them up and set them aside. If they do not match, turn them back over so you can no longer see what they are, leaving them in their original position.

Turn over another card and try to find the one that matches it.

Continue until you have matched and removed all the cards.

How long did it take you? With practice, your concentration will improve and you will be able to remember the cards you've turned over and clear the deck more quickly.

	Time
1st Round	
2nd Round	
3rd Round	
4th Round	
5th Round	

You can also play this game with a partner. If you make a match, you keep the cards you matched and go again. If you do not, you turn the cards back over and your opponent gets a turn. Whoever ends up with the most pairs wins.

you usually put on your right shoe first, begin with your left foot (in your left shoe, of course).

Experience something new for breakfast. If you always breakfast at home, eat out once in a while. As most people are not fully alert first thing in the morning, it is easier to program new ideas into your morning, when you're receptive but a little out of it. Sample different kinds of cereal, fresh fruit, yogurt, minced soy (it really is delicious), or a cooked breakfast. Do this at least once a week and on a different day each week. Carry this over into your other meals. When eating out, if you don't feel adventurous enough to try a new main course, then order a different starter. Pay attention to smells and textures as well. You will be simultaneously expanding your sensory abilities and learning new things.

Going to work a different way will give you a new awareness of your environment. You will discover roads you didn't know existed. You will pass by businesses whose services you will use. Better still, you may find a new company you can do business with. If you always drive, take the bus. If you always take the bus, take a subway or train. You will be amazed at the different perspective you can achieve.

Pick up a magazine in an area in which you have no particular interest. A keen golfer might get a magazine on knitting, or a middle-aged lady might get one on bodybuilding. You get the idea. Now read the magazine and create connections that relate to you specifically. At times one idea or even one word may hit you, which might suggest another idea or word in your mind, which could solve a totally unrelated problem for you. So on your next plane journey, buy a magazine at the airport, one you would normally never even glance at. Allow it to speak to you. Now read it upside down . . . yes, get those synapses firing and rewiring like crazy.

While we're on the topic of speech, increase your word knowledge. When you come across a new word, or a word you aren't really sure about, look it up in the dictionary. Make a point of using that word as soon as you learn it. Check it out in the thesaurus as well and find words with the same meaning. That way, each new word you learn will bring two or three new words into your active vocabulary. This will also help you think more clearly and concisely, and to reflect more kindly on all those English teachers who kept drilling you all those years.

Tackle that one project you've been putting off first thing in the morning. Whether that involves writing letters or doing your daily workout, just do it instead of procrastinating yet again. By tackling it immediately you have put the most difficult task of the day behind you, and all the rest is plain sailing, especially if you've programmed yourself for success the preceding night.

Before you go to bed, take thirty seconds to program yourself for the next day. Your instructions to yourself might read: "When the clock sounds off in the morning, I will sit straight up in bed, saying it's a great day to get up and get at them. I will climb out of the end of the bed. I will dress myself starting with my socks and I see myself having completed my tax return." One note—you must visualize this entire scene happening in your mind. But now, how hard can it be to see yourself signing that tax return or completing that letter? See? You're halfway there!

PROBLEM-SOLVING TECHNIQUE

Hillary Clinton summons up Eleanor Roosevelt and talks to her when grappling with issues in the political arena. Though Eleanor's part of the conversation is imaginary, Hillary knows so much about her hero that she can figure out what her take would be, and in effect get a second opinion. General Patton did the same with Hannibal. By looking at our lives—and our problems—in a whole new way, we not only expand our world but we also clarify the questions and find solutions. The next time you're faced with a dilemma, try this.

CONVERSING WITH THE DEAD

This is not what you think. Rather it is an exercise in creativity. Decide what genius from history you want to advise you and what your problem or question is. Sit back, relax, and take a few deep breaths. Close your eyes and see yourself in a tranquil state, perhaps in a beautiful garden or in a scene from a painting. Describe aloud what you see. Explore the scene. Now your visitor arrives to see you. Describe him (or her) in full detail, including appearance, mannerisms, clothing, etc. Imagine entering that person like a suit of armor.

You are now looking out through his eyes. Describe out loud what he sees. It may be the same scene or a different one. Let the images flow. Now turn your thoughts to the question. Let your borrowed genius look it over. Again describe out loud what he sees.

There was a point in his life when his genius was at its peak. Allow yourself to feel this. Feel how he felt. Describe it aloud. You are now nearly ready to come back to yourself. Visualize a full-length mirror in front of you and you see his reflection in it. Allow the mirror to fade away.

He is now standing in front of you. He has his own head back. You are again two separate beings. Ask him your question. What does he want to tell you? You will be surprised by his advice!

As crazy as this may sound, it's a great way to broaden your outlook or find solutions to problems. Your genius doesn't have to be a historical figure. I speak to my father who's been dead for 25 years. I don't communicate with the dead at all, but rather I dive into his knowledge and his wisdom by asking him questions. I put my mind in a state to see things through a different perspective,

MIND BUILDER

Stretch your mind by only reading the left-hand page of a novel. Your expanding brainpower will fill in the blanks, and you'll avoid the redundancies.

through a perspective of how he saw the world, which was a different way than how I see the world.

I'll ask, "Do I concentrate too much on the financial aspect of things?" I know him well enough to know his answer. "When I began my life, I made so little money it isn't funny. We had to raise a family." I'll reply, "Yeah, Dad, but it killed you so young, because you worked so hard and you made so little." In this way, you begin having this dialogue, about the nature of life and death and loss. When it's finished, you are somewhat spent, but you've also gone through a dialectic that you wouldn't have gone through if you were thinking and arguing with yourself.

It's all up to you. Want a mental Porsche instead of a beat-up Chevy? Don't settle for the first solution to a problem, or a second-rate mind. Practice this week's memory exercises again and again. Then break out of the mental box you've built around your brain: Eat dessert first!

CHAPTER 8

PLAY (KEY 6)

PENDULUM POWER

Every thought has a physical manifestation that can translate into movement, which explains nonverbal communication as well as the power of the pendulum. You can actually *see* the power of your mind at work when you use a pendulum to problem-solve. Of the many mind tools I've introduced you to in this book, the one that people resist most at first is the intuitive pendulum. There is something about using a physical object that my students find disconcerting. Once they try it, however, they become devotees because it enables them to take advantage of the body-mind connection in a whole new way by mining the physical manifestations of the mind as revealed by the motion of the pendulum to answer questions and tap into the subconscious.

I first saw a pendulum being used by a stranger who accurately located buried objects. It was shown to me by an old man who learned it in Eastern Europe. He would bury coins in holes in the backyard. Months later, he would use the pendulum to find them again. I've also seen divining rods—which operate on the same principle as a pendulum—used on farms in Galveston, Texas, to find water, and watched the rod swing down over an underground water source. I even tried it in a sandbox with a buried cup of water.

I have been fascinated by pendulums ever since. I've read every-thing I could find on the subject and have used one for years and years. And I can sum up all that learning in two words: It works. As I was finishing writing this book, a man came up to me and said, "You don't know me, but my wife and I went to a seminar about finding lost objects given by a woman whom you taught. She showed us the pendulum technique. Not long after, my wife lost her gold ring and used the pendulum to find it."

Now those powers are in your hands. In the midst of all these mental gymnastics, which can seem daunting and even impossible to do, a pendulum gives even the newest beginner an easy way to crack open the first secrets of the mind. Which explains why the pendulum has been used as a tool for the exploration of human intuition and psyche for as long as humans have existed. It requires no great technological skill to make a pendulum; even the most primitive of cultures can—and have—constructed them. Almost anything can be used: bone, leather, hair, crystal, wood, coral, ivory, clay, seashells, thread. So you can buy a pendulum or simply make your own. I own a few dozen different pendulums and am always on the lookout for some new unique object to suspend from a cord, chain, thread, or string.

All cultures have a history of magic and healing of some sort. Someplace in nearly all of these folk tales and bits of great-grand-motherly wisdom, a pendulum appears.

The predictive use of the pendulum seems to have originated in northern Europe and Great Britain. A pregnant young woman is advised to tie her wedding ring to a long strand of her hair. She suspends this pendulum over one upturned palm and asks herself the sex of the child she's carrying. It eventually responds by swing-ing back and forth for a male child or swinging in a circle for a female. Other tales instruct that the pendulum be held only in the left hand, or over the woman's abdomen or the wrist. Some specify that her house key be used instead of her ring. Still others specify that a favorite sewing needle tied to a thread be used.

An anthropological text described how a Siberian shaman used a piece of carved bone tied to a thin strip of soft leather to discover where the hunting would be best for the wandering tribe. As this method had been handed down from father shaman to son shaman for many generations, it must have repeatedly worked well for them. A shaman who couldn't find food for his wandering tribe of hunters would not remain shaman for long!

I've read of a similar pendulum test used by an African tribe to discover who was stealing a tribal member's food.

There are also many references to water being located this way—not only by walking about in the fields and forests but also by suspending the pendulum over a map of the area! Hopeful gold and oil prospectors have successfully used similar methods in their search for riches.

SWING ALONG

Whether you use the pendulum to find an answer or an object, or to simply free up your mind, remember that the pendulum is not some supernatural thing, but rather your thoughts amplified and made visible. That's the key. Nothing the pendulum does is outside your control. The pendulum is neither occult nor supernatural. It is a tool whose motion is based on ideo-motor response (a thought triggering a physical response). What happens is merely controlled by your subconscious instead of your conscious mind. Using a pendulum is one way to calibrate and visualize those physical movements..

Though I can't explain why a pendulum poised over a map could yield information about water sources, I do know from personal experience and study that this device can be a quick route to tapping into your subconscious mind and unleashing its potential. I'm actually such a fan that I have kept research notes of my various experiments over weeks or months in an attempt to make some more scientific sense of how a pendulum can—or cannot—be used.

But now it's time for you to see for yourself.

Go to your refrigerator and take out a lemon (sour). Grab four packets of sugar (sweet). Lay them out on a table in a straight line. Place the lemon at whatever position you choose. Now, place the pendulum over each item in the line. When it's over the sugar packets, the movement should be similar. But when it's placed over the lemon, you will notice a different movement beginning to occur.

You can repeat this experiment with other items that offer stark contrast. For example, an excellent test involves photographs. Get a magazine with plenty of pictures. Cut out four pictures of living people and one picture of someone who has died. Place them in a row. When you get to the person who has passed on, you will notice the pendulum act up.

What's going on here? The pendulum isn't picking up some electromagnetic energy from the lemon. The pendulum has no power to move on its own accord. It's just an object tied to a string. You're the one creating the movement. The pendulum simply acts as the physical manifestation of your thoughts. And therein lies its beauty.

PENDULUM MINDSCRIPT

The pendulum is its own mindscript because your mind is what dictates its movement. So instead of presenting an additional mindscript here, I will simply remind you to close your eyes before trying each of the exercises in this chapter and allow yourself to enter the total relaxed state. Don't forget to record what happens in your learning log.

It's All in Your Head

You—and by extension, the pendulum—are the one who reacts differently to the different thought manifestations of your mind. Having asked someone to hold something, for example, I must discern which hand it's in. So I put a pendulum over one of her hands and then over the other. The pendulum swings back and forth over both, but on this occasion swings more when over the left hand. So I say, "The object is in that hand," and I'm correct. I can do this again and again, and be right every time.

What's happening? I suspect that I am seeing either a subtle difference between the two hands, or in the way the person holding the object is looking at her left hand rather than her right. Having picked up these clues that I'm consciously not even aware of, I make the pendulum swing more over one hand than the other.

Finding lost objects with a pendulum is another way to tap that inner mind connection. When something goes missing, in most cases it's simply a case of forgetting where we left it. I once had a client ask me how she could find her lost watch, bracelet, and rings. I instructed her to use a pendulum and a simple yes-no card. She asked herself questions (such as *Did I leave my jewelry at the gym? Did I leave my jewelry in the kitchen?*) while holding the pendulum over the yes-no card. Based on the information provided by the pendulum, she managed to narrow down the possibilities of where the lost items could be. She eventually found them outside on a low garden wall; she had taken them off to work in the garden.

Did the pendulum itself find them for her? Of course not. On some level she "knew" where they were—after all, she had put them there. She simply needed a way to tap her unconscious in

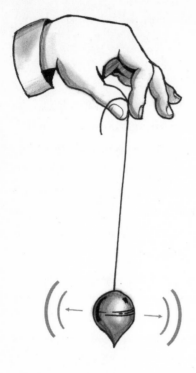

order to bring to the surface of her mind the memory of taking them off.

Even if you've lost something without merely misplacing it, your subconscious almost always harbors clues as to how and where the object was lost. While you were walking down the street, you didn't notice the *ping* as your earring fell to the sidewalk, but your subconscious heard it. With the aid of the pendulum and that simple yes-no card, you may be able to reconstruct where and when you lost that earring.

Keep in mind that you only know what you know. In other words, if it's not in your subconscious, you are not going to suddenly divine where something is, pendulum or no pendulum. That's why it's critical that the person who lost the object conduct the experiment. If *I* had manipulated the pendulum and asked questions about the jewelry that was misplaced in the garden or that dropped earring, there would be no information for the pendulum to access. So I could have never been successful in recovering those items using this method, though I sure could find those reading glasses I put down that seem to have disappeared.

The varied ways you can use a pendulum are practically endless. Playing around with this simple practice script will get you started. Hold the pendulum between your thumb and index finger. Hold it so it's suspended about 2 inches above the middle of the yes/no/not sure circle in the Appendix on page 217. Rest your elbow on the table, or whatever surface you are using. Take a couple of slow deep breaths and then breathe normally. Relax your mind.

Think of the *yes* direction, i.e., up and down. It may take a few seconds or a minute but the pendulum will start moving up and down, as if you were nodding your head, signifying *yes*.

Now concentrate on the *no* direction, i.e., sideways. Think as hard as you can. The pendulum will begin moving side to side, as if you were shaking your head *no*.

Concentrate on the *not sure* direction, i.e., a circle, and watch as the pendulum starts revolving in a circular motion. It may rotate clockwise or counterclockwise.

The key to making it work is to focus all your attention. Picture the pendulum moving in the direction you are concentrating on. See it moving. After you've completed these warm-up exercises, you can move on to the next exercise.

Ready to find those missing car keys? Assuming someone else (like your teenager or your mate) hasn't taken them, your subconscious mind remembers where you put them, even if your conscious mind does not. So ask the pendulum where your keys are, just as our gardener asked about her jewelry. Remember to phrase your questions in *yes* or *no* form. For example, you might ask: *Are the keys in the bedroom? Are they in the living room?* If you get a yes to one of the rooms, ask the pendulum more questions to narrow the search: *Are they in the back of the room? Are they in a drawer?*

You get the idea.

PERSONAL Q & A'S

The most fascinating and often-used exercise with the pendulum is to answer questions of a personal nature—you know, the ones that drive us all nuts. By tapping into your subconscious mind, you can often arrive at the correct decision instantly instead of tormenting yourself with all that indecision. How? Because the pendulum can delve straight into your subconscious and unleash the answer that lies in your heart.

Take a moment and think of a question you would like to know the answer to. It might relate to a situation you are currently involved in, or some aspect of your future. It must be a question that can be answered by a *yes* or *no*, which only makes sense since a pendulum, which has no power of its own, clearly lacks oratory skills as well.

Below you'll see five separate icons. Each represents a different category of your life. The subjects are:

- Relationships
- Home & Family
- Money & Career $
- Travel
- Category of Your Choosing (Your Category)   **?**

Once you have a question in mind, pick the category image it falls into. In other words, if your question concerns a person that you're dating, you would use the Relationship category. If your question is about your job, you'd use the Money & Career category. If you have a question that does not fall into the first four categories, you'd use the Your Category picture.

For example, if your question is *Will I enjoy the movie tonight?*, you'd use the Your Category picture because that really isn't related to the other categories (although if you were going to the movie with a date, then you'd probably use the Relationship category).

Hold the pendulum by the end of the cord between your thumb and index finger. Position the pendulum in the middle of the circle with the + running through it, about 2 inches above the picture. Rest your elbow on the surface. Focus your complete attention on your question. Now let the pendulum take its course.

MIND BUILDER

Pendulums are all about using tools to tap into our subconscious. Using a tool for a purpose other than that for which it was originally designed will help you take a creative and perception-broadening leap that will develop your conscious mind as well.

If the pendulum doesn't move at all or if it goes in a circle, it means that the answer is unclear at the present. Rephrasing the question and asking it again can help. If the pendulum continues to demonstrate uncertainty, proceed with another question and come back to your initial query later or another day.

You can ask the pendulum as many questions as you like. Just remember to change subject categories when switching from a question about relationships to one about your job.

THE HUMAN PENDULUM

A pendulum doesn't have to be a bob and a bit of string. Our bodies and minds react to thoughts, both spoken and silent. Haven't you ever observed someone yawn and then a few seconds later felt the urge to yawn as well?

Here's a neat experiment that shows you how a thought can affect someone without them knowing it. You will need at least five people to try this out.

Designate one person to be the Human Pendulum, i.e., the thought receiver. Send that person out of the room for a moment. After she leaves, you must all decide on one direction that you want that person to sway.

There are four possibilities: forward, backward, to the left side, to the right side. Once you've decided on the direction, call the receiver back into the room.

The four of you stand in a circle around the receiver. One of you is in front of her, one in back, one on the left side, and one on the right side. The receiver stands up straight, head facing forward. Her feet are close together.

The person in front places each hand on each shoulder of the receiver. The person in back also places their hands on the receiver's shoulders, as do the two people at each side. Move in close so your arms are bent in.

Have the receiver close her eyes. Tell her you are all going to concentrate on the direction you want her to sway. Reassure her that she can't fall because you're all around her.

Now the four of you who are holding onto her must focus all your concentration on willing her to sway in the one direction you decided on. See her swaying in that direction, like a pendulum, and project that single thought to her.

The receiver must strive to pick up your thoughts. She must relax her mind and think of nothing. When she feels the urge to sway in a particular direction, she must not resist. And when she finally does sway, notice the direction and then support her so she doesn't fall.

Try the test at least four times, then switch so that each of you plays the role of the receiver. If the receiver sways in the correct direction one out of four times, that's average. More than that is above average.

PENDULUM ORBS

One of the drawbacks to the yes-no answers experiments is that you're limited to a binary format. That's not to say it's bad, it's just that in some situations, you may want more information than a simple yes or no can provide.

That's where the Pendulum Orbs come in. In the Appendix on pages 218 to 222, you will find diagrams that enable you to zero in

MIND TOOLS

Can you read another person's thoughts with the help of a pendulum?

Get a partner. Designate which one will be the thought receiver and which one will be the thought sender. The receiver holds the pendulum over the circle as in the first pendulum picture. The sender lightly holds the receiver's wrist—the one from which the pendulum is suspended.

Now, the sender begins to concentrate on either the up and down direction (yes), the sideways direction (no), or the circular direction (not sure). Very shortly, the pendulum will begin to move in one of those three directions. When it does, tell the receiver if that was the correct direction or not.

Take turns being the receiver and sender. Try it at least 10 times each. If you get the correct direction three times out of 10, that's average. Four to five is above average, and more than five is great. Keep practicing. You can then ask personal questions that relate to the receiver. But be warned, you may get answers that surprise you!

	PERSON 1		PERSON 2	
	Correct	Incorrect	Correct	Incorrect
1				
2				
3				
4				
5				
6				
7				
8				
9				
10				

on specifics, including names, dates, numbers, letters, days of the week, months of the year, and more. You are only limited by your imagination.

Here's how to use the Orbs. Maybe you want to know what day of the week is best to start a project. Flip to the Days of the Week Orb in the Appendix. Turn the book sideways. Hold the pendulum over the middle of the circle. Concentrate on your question. When the pendulum starts swinging over a particular day, you've got your answer!

GOOD VIBRATIONS

Objects can also clue us in to the personality and emotional state of their owner, which you—and by extension the pendulum—can pick up on. Some people believe personal things can carry vibrations— for lack of a better word—that are indicative of the person for whom the object has an emotional meaning. If you've ever held on to someone else's watch, or their necklace, and had feelings about it, you may have experienced psychometry. Dr. J. Buchanan, a scientist who spent many years investigating this intriguing subject, coined the word in 1842.

Psychometry does not involve the supernatural or occult but is based on the premise that everything radiates vibrations, and most people, with practice, are able to sense them. Many think the vibrations are really just a hypersensitivity to the kinds of nonverbal cues we examined earlier. They may be right. Your mind makes assumptions and follows paths it feels comfortable with, so it tends to make choices, close off certain avenues, and open up others. I was once handed a rock and asked to "read" it. For whatever reason, my reaction to the rock was, "You thought you were in danger, but you're not." Now, I don't know exactly which signals led me to this conclusion, but it could be argued that my mind zeroed in on this explanation because there weren't many other reasons for this ordinary-looking rock to carry an emotional charge heavy enough for someone to hand it to me for a "reading." It turned out that the rock had been thrown through the window of the man's house, and that he had felt himself threatened but that the threat had since dissipated. So whether my response was triggered by the vibrations of the rock or the logical leaps my mind can make, I can't say. Either way, the rock itself played a role as well.

READING ME & YOU

As you know, psychometry relies on simply taking an object that belongs to a person and describing the feelings you perceive about it. Since, according to the theory behind psychometry, our personality rubs off on the objects that we keep with us and that we are in contact with, by holding the object, you can tap into the owner's personality as well as his past and present. Psychometry is just another tool for reading the world around you and the people in it in order to make the most of your interactions. Use it as you do every other mind tool in this book, in conjunction with each other and as pieces of an overall package of tools.

So, how do you go about reading a person by psychometry? Well, you simply try it. Get a group of people together. You are going to try to read each other by holding onto objects that are personal to them. Now, obviously, a problem arises. You probably know most of the people in your group, as it is likely they are your friends and/or family. Here's how to get around that:

Get some plain envelopes. Give one to each person. Tell them to take out an object that they own and—without showing it to anyone—place it in the envelope and seal it. No photos of themselves are allowed, for obvious reasons. Then have one person collect all the envelopes and mix them up. Take one envelope, open it up, and hold the object in your hand. Close your eyes; feel the texture of the object. Start describing whatever pops into your mind. Don't even think. Just start talking, let the information flow out.

It will feel awkward the first time you try it. Don't be discouraged. Describe what you feel is the personality of the object's owner. Describe what you sense is her history, places she's gone, situations she's been through, what's going on now, even her future. Whatever comes to mind. Once you've finished, have the owner identify herself and tell you if what you said makes sense. In most cases, you'll be amazed by the direct hits you score.

Pass the envelopes to the next person. Have him open an envelope and begin describing the owner. Some things that are described may make no sense to the owner, but will later on, upon reflection. If you should, by chance, choose your own object, remove it from the envelope and select another.

As you progress, you can begin reading people in social situations whom you genuinely don't know. Have them hand you a personal item and off you go. This game is absolutely fascinating once you get the hang of it. It's a superb way to further develop your nonverbal sensitivities. And it's not a bad way to break the ice at parties, either.

CHAPTER 9

STILL PLAY—IT'S ALL IN YOUR MIND

HAVE FUN GROWING YOUR NEW MENTAL POWERS

We've seen it again and again—your mind influences your world. In this last chapter, I'll give you the final keys to unlock your master mind, as well as a few more tips that will help you put together and use symphonically all you've learned. Then we'll test that new *master mind of yours* to see just what you can do now that you couldn't before.

From nonverbal communication to ideo-motor movements like those of the pendulum, we are surrounded by proof of the mental power we all possess. But that's just the tip of the iceberg. You have to be ready for things to happen. As Albert Einstein, a believer in intuitive powers, said, "Chance favors the prepared mind."

Take the example of this oh-so-New-York story from my own life. We were living in a tiny apartment on Manhattan's Upper West Side. Our family had been expanding, my shows were successful, and real estate values had stabilized. We were ready to move someplace larger. Through a series of typical New York events, we found that we had sold our old apartment without having secured a new one. Tova scoured the papers but found nothing that met our needs. Time was running out. Within a matter of weeks we would have to hand over the keys of our current apartment and would be stuck moving to a hotel. Several places presented themselves. They weren't perfect, but they were available and we were about to be homeless. Still, Tova's inner voice told her they were not *it*.

Placing herself in a mental frame of opportunity, she refused to settle. Instead, she focused on positive thoughts and visualized the type of layout needed. Shortly thereafter, a friend of ours visited a family that was relocating out of the city. Without even knowing that we were looking to move, she called Tova to tell her about the place they were selling . . . which proved perfect. We still live there today.

Optimism, positive thoughts, friendship, homework, and intuitive tenacity all paid off. So did the fact that Tova could see in her mind what she wanted. And that's exactly what she got. You have to put yourself in a position to be lucky—to position yourself to let things happen, have the patience to let them happen at their own pace, and have confidence that the universe will indeed provide.

Fine-tuning your perspective, which is what this book is mainly about, is like cleaning a window or a mirror. Suddenly you can really see what's out there, and see others for what they really are. The quickest way to fog that glass up, however, is to let your emotions form the basis for your analysis of the world around you. Instead, rely on what you've learned in this book to help you clearly identify what's really happening, so that you can react in a manner that will give you the edge.

"The greatest discovery of my generation is that human beings, by changing the inner attitudes of their minds, can change the outer aspects of their lives," proclaimed psychologist and philosopher William James (1842–1910). This certainly presents a good argument for free will. It also shows us the power of our minds. Positive thinking makes you healthier and can even make you heal faster.

I've seen this work especially well with kids. The doctor uses a Magic Marker to color a wart and explains to the child that the wart will decrease in size and eventually disappear as the ink wears off. That suggestion is often enough to make that happen because the child believes without reservations that the doctor knows what he's talking about. Unfortunately, this method doesn't work with adults—perhaps because we lack the total trust in doctors that children usually have. Phenomena like the placebo effect, however, are well-documented evidence of the power of suggestion.

In many ways, you become what you think. Creative visualization is built on James' type of thinking. If you think about what you'd like to achieve in your life, you can do just that. For example, if you want to own a brand-new car, picture yourself in that car, happily driving it off the lot and waving to your friends as you drive it home. Be aware that using this technique works best when you place yourself in the picture. If you just picture a beautiful, empty car, it will stay that way, and so will your driveway.

SENSORY RELAXATION MINDSCRIPT

By now you probably realize that relaxation ultimately is the key to achieving a master mind. So I'm going to present you with one last mindscript to help you with relaxation. I've saved it for the end because it brings in so much of what we've learned about sensory perception. I also want to remind you that not everything works for everyone. So even if the other relaxation mindscripts haven't worked for you, give this one a try. It just may prove the answer.

The Magic of Your Mind

Sit down and make yourself comfortable. Close your eyes.

Imagine yourself at the top of a beautiful staircase. Examine it in detail in your mind. What is it made of? Does it have a banister or handrail? Is it indoors or outdoors?

This staircase can have steps leading down to the most comfortable and relaxing place you can imagine. Decide now in your mind what sort of a place this will be. For instance, you may choose a garden, a beach, or a cozy room with a comfortable armchair by the fire. It could be a place you have been to before or one you create in your imagination. Make it every bit as beautiful as you would like it to be.

In a few moments, as you count yourself down these steps in your mind, you can become more relaxed and at ease with each step you take.

Count yourself down the steps from 1 to 20 in time with each or every second out breath (exhalation). This can have the effect of helping to slow and steady the breathing pattern even further.

Intersperse suggestions for relaxation throughout. For instance, "As I continue my descent to this beautiful place, a feeling of deep calm can seep through to the very core of my being," or "When I reach the last step, I can feel wonderfully relaxed and comfortable."

Having reached the bottom of the staircase, you now find yourself in that special place you have chosen. Explore its beauty, using all your senses in your imagination. Firstly, you may wish to use your sense of sight by visualizing this place in detail in your mind. Then move through your other senses by smelling, touching, hearing, and even tasting what surrounds you, if appropriate. Make everything as real as possible in your mind so that you can almost feel you are actually there.

Find somewhere comfortable to sit in this scene, a spot where you can work with the suggestions and imagery of your choice.

To come out of this script, simply reverse the way you came in. Count yourself back up the steps from 20 to 1, this time counting on each or every second in breath (inhalation). This will help you to become progressively more alert as you approach the top of the staircase in your mind.

Suggest that when you open your eyes you can feel refreshed, calm, and alert. Open your eyes. Have a nice stretch!

During the preceding exercises you may have experienced subtle or even dramatic physical and psychological changes. For instance, you may have become aware of feelings of heaviness, lightness, warmth, tingling sensations, or numbness. You may also have found that you became completely absorbed in feelings of relaxation. Perhaps you even experienced some time distortion whereby you thought your time in your thoughts was longer or shorter than it actually was. All these are common and perfectly normal experiences of the hypnotic state. However, it does not need to become a matter of concern if you did not experience any of the above. As previously stated, each person experiences this self-talk in their own personal way. What is of prime importance is that you have taken some time to relax and work positively on yourself to your benefit.

Visualization is a control tool of great potency. I've found that my students who are clearest about what they want to create achieve their goals much more quickly. Those who feel unsure of their goals, feel they don't deserve them, or believe they may be unattainable slow down or even halt the process of manifesting their desires.

JUST SEE IT TO BELIEVE IT

To encourage creative visualization, see your mind as a blank movie, TV, or computer screen. Let an image of anything at all begin to form. Let your mind create it and make it meaningful. Try to see it as clearly as you can, as if it were right in front of you. Now morph it in your mind into another image. Finally, bring it back to a formless state. You may be surprised to find that you have visualized something that is actually taking place somewhere else.

Part of visualization involves mentally living through an activity to prepare your brain for the real activity. Before I begin any project, I take time to sit down and imagine how I want things to go. In essence, I'm rehearsing my task by visualizing it.

You can use visualization for any endeavor. As I mentioned before, I've had the opportunity to coach many athletes (as well as actors, writers, and artists) on how to develop superior abilities through mental control and imagery. I have guided all-star football players like Jason Sehorn and Michael Strahan in picking up the cues of the opposition, pain control, and the secrets of elongated time—slowing down your impression of the world around you in order to see fast-moving events in slow motion. For the latter, I taught them to visualize a feather falling. Think about it. A falling feather is one of the few things in nature that happens in real time but appears to be happening in slow motion. If everyone around you is the falling feather, they are still in real time but they are moving very slowly. You, on the other hand, are also in real time but moving at the speed you choose. Get it? They're slow, you're fast. Nothing has changed aside from your perception of how you move. Except now you're winning the game.

HELP YOURSELF

Remember, only a small part of our mental activity takes place in ordinary consciousness. The subconscious is vast, but with organization and practice, it can be brought to heel. Our perceptions, the ones that we store in our subconscious, are heavily influenced by our beliefs. In turn, our beliefs are influenced by suggestions we receive, especially those regularly repeated. So give yourself some good suggestions—use affirmations such as "I am a great salesman" or "I like myself" on a daily basis and you will help change your self-image for the better.

My older brother was usually not a great student. But throughout his life, he embraced everything with an "I can do this" approach. He repeated that internal message to himself constantly. Today, he is a brilliant CEO of one of the largest bureaus of Jewish education in the country.

Though many people are quick to scoff at affirmations (I still feel like making some wisecracks), all that stops once they give them a try because they work. Positive verbal expressions send a message to your mind indicating what you want to achieve. And that sets it up for delivering the goods. I always thought I'd pass exams. I always knew I'd be successful in interviews. It was a matter of attitude. You simply think things will work. And in most cases, they do. If they don't, affirmations will help you seize the opportunity to open yourself up to new possibilities.

Think of it this way: A guy is walking along and he sees a series of targets drawn on the wall, each with an arrow in the bull's-eye. He says to the archer, "Wow, did you hit all those targets?" And the archer replies, "No, first I shoot the arrow, then I draw the target." That's what this type of affirmation is about—mentally putting yourself in a situation and drawing the results around it that you want.

When you choose a positive statement, always use the present tense, so that your changes can take place now, rather than some time in the far-off future. For example, say *I am open to my intuition and easily act on its wisdom*, instead of *I will be open to my intuition*. Say it aloud so that your ears experience the positive sounds, too. And remember, just as positive affirmations will help you improve your situation, negative thoughts that you repeat often work with the same efficacy to deliver exactly what you don't want.

Here's an exercise to get you in touch with what motivates you.

1. Bring to mind a time in your life when you received something you *really* wanted. This could be a career change, a relationship,

a house, a car, a family, or anything else of your choosing. Write this down.

2. What were the factors that made you successful in achieving this goal? Did you take action? Did you pray? Did you just think you were lucky? Did you have to work hard to get it? Did you have to let go of trying to get it to happen? Write down anything that comes to mind about this.

3. What were the obstacles involved in achieving this goal? Were you discouraged? Did friends and family tell you not to do it? Was there a block that you had to overcome in yourself first? Write anything that comes to mind about this.

4. Imagine that you have a wise being looking out for you. This being knows you want more prosperity, peace, love, success, and ease in your life. Close your eyes and ask this wise being what you should do to bring more of these qualities into your life. Ask your wise being what you should do when you feel discouraged.

Getting in touch with why you're blocked and what you need to do to remain motivated can help you immensely. You can learn much about yourself by understanding why you aren't moving forward. Remember, your intuition is always giving you an opportunity to learn.

Your mind is an amazing thing. The biological processes of our brain are exceedingly complex, with new revelations uncovered almost daily. What we do know is that we have two upper brains that operate, for the most part, with different abilities and potentials. The two sides of your brain, the left and right cortex, are linked with a marvelously complex series of nerve fibers. In most people the left cortex deals with logic, words, analysis, and other so-called academic activities. The right cortex deals with things like imagination, color, daydreaming, and spatial awareness. With some simple techniques we can begin to take control of the abilities we all share.

Recent developments show that there are far more connections and redundancies between the two sides than we ever thought. In order to power up our minds we need to strengthen both halves as a whole. Stimulating both sides may be the best way to maximize our inherent capacities. Thus learning, mental exercise, games, and human interaction all play a role in giving the brain greater flexibility. If we live in either half of the brain, we experience only half of the world.

CHANGE YOUR MOOD JUST LIKE THAT

Just as we can use the power of our minds to change our external lives, we can consciously impact our internal lives simply by changing our sensory input. It's true. Our senses help us deal with the physical properties of the world around us. Recent research indicates that by changing our sensory input, we can change our mood—and a lot more safely than all those chemical or even herbal substances on the market.

Here are five mood elevators based on each of your five senses.

- **Sight:** Confusion makes us uneasy. Visualizing input that is relaxing will put you in a relaxed/enhanced mental mood. Nature works for many people. That's why looking at trees, fields, a brook, or even the sky will put your mind in a mellow state. Colors, too, impact mood. Blue and bubble gum are relaxing colors. Need a pick-me-up? Try a dose of vibrant reds and purples. Bright colors like yellow can jump-start creativity. Avoid orange—it actually acts as an irritant.

- **Sound:** Most of us know how quickly a noise (or noise in general) can put us in a foul mood. Very few people are comfortable with jackhammering going on outside their home. And how ready were you to do physical damage the last time a car alarm in your neighborhood went off and wouldn't stop?

Of course, this also means that good sounds give us good emotions. We've already explored how music can relax or rejuvenate you. Well, it can energize you as well. Do the dishes to Radiohead, build furniture to hip-hop musicals. Choose the right piece of music to fit your taste, and its rhythm and pacing will help engender the frame of mind you're seeking. Have a big meeting coming up and you're sick to your stomach? Try a classical piece of music or a Led Zeppelin ballad to help calm your butterflies. In romance, Ravel's *Bolero* does the trick for a good many of us.

You'll also find that the sounds of nature provide bliss—a babbling brook or a bird in a tree are both mood-enhancing experiences. So that walk that you took earlier to see the trees and the sky didn't just rely on visual stimuli to make you feel better but on helpful auditory input as well. As long as you avoided the chainsaw, that is.

- **Smell:** This underrated and underutilized sense can further impact our emotional state. We're wired to enjoy some smells and dislike others. That rotting meat you didn't see at the back of the fridge all last month, for example, doesn't just challenge your sensibilities, it serves as a warning. Even an infant recognizes odors and screws up his face when he smells something bad. Conversely, agreeable scents trigger pleasure, though we often don't recognize—or take advantage—of that. Lavender has a surprisingly soothing effect. You'll want to avoid patchouli, however, as well as tobacco smoke, which in general works against you.

Once you know which smells work for you, you can use them to lift your emotional state. For some, smells from their childhood trigger positive feelings. Others respond to the aroma of yeasty bread or freshly mowed grass or the fragrance of fresh fruit. Ozone—that smell of electricity in the air before a thunderstorm— is also a powerful mood enhancer. But since ozone is also generated by shower water, you don't have to be weather-dependent for an uplifting ozone fix. Just turn on the tap and hop on in. You'll come out feeling invigorated not just because of the water but also because of the ionization of the air particles that you smell as the water pours over your body.

- **Taste:** Most of us know all too well how good certain tastes can make us feel. Whether chocolate or pasta Alfredo do it for you, your favorite foods are almost guaranteed to make you feel like a million bucks while you're eating them, even if you want to kill yourself later because of your ever-expanding girth. It's not just the *taste* of foods like gelato or triple-cream Brie, either—it's the way they feel in the mouth and the way they wrap around your tongue that heighten the whole eating experience. A variety of textures makes us most enthused—i.e., enjoying crunchy foods (popcorn, nuts, chips) with fatty emulsion on the tongue (dip, meat, butter, ice cream). Combining sweet and sour tastes also works well.

- **Touch:** Imagine that your fingers are vacuum cleaners or hypersensitive antennae as you stroke your hair, your face, your pants, grass and pick up what those things feel like. You can make yourself feel good in a snap simply by sensitizing yourself to the texture of materials and then touching them often. Silk or satin sheets are a luxury—just their memory will keep a smile on your face.

Human touch is remarkably potent. When somebody's in pain, just hug them. Likewise, if you're feeling sad, find someone to hug you. The skin has so many nerve endings that contact enhances

MIND TOOLS

Are you the master of your mind yet? Now that your ability to perceive the world around you is at an all-time high and your antenna is way up, you notice more than you ever have on all levels, and the world is your oyster. Or is it?

It's time to find out how much you've grown on the mental front. If you're not happy with the results, go back through the book starting with Chapter 1 and practice all the exercises, then try again. Remember, it took me a lifetime to develop these skills; you need to be patient and persistent in your mental workouts.

1. Have you tried recently to get someone to do what you want and did it work?
2. Do you tend to think and observe at a superficial or a profound level? How do you know?
3. Have you been successful at trying to read someone's thoughts?
4. Do you relax easily?
5. Is your stress level low or high?
6. Do you consider yourself a creative person?
7. Are you an imaginative problem-solver?
8. Are you observant when it comes to detail?
9. Do you read people correctly? How do you know?

how we feel. The Harlow experiments in the 1960s and 1970s showed us that touch can even impact our physical development. In this famous research, baby monkeys raised on terry cloth frames grew larger than those raised on wire frames. The lack of a comforting texture made the difference. That's why, these days, incubated newborns are placed on ultra-touchable sheepskin.

The impact of touch also explains why pets (perhaps with the exception of snakes and lizards) are such powerful emotional elevators. Not only do you have a furry body to stroke, the animal

10. How attuned are you to nonverbal communication?
11. Are you aware of the messages that your body language—and even choice of clothing and accessories—says about you?
12. Have you ever tried to ascertain whether or not a person was lying to you? Were you successful?
13. Have you successfully influenced someone's choice or changed how they thought about an issue?
14. Do you exercise your mind?
15. Can you remember names easily? How about facts and figures?
16. Are you intuitive when it comes to people and events?
17. Have you ever had a precognitive (predictive) experience?
18. Can you sense danger?
19. Do you have a knack for finding misplaced or lost items?
20. Have you ever tried alternative approaches to solving a problem?
21. Do you remember your dreams?
22. Can you use visualization to try to get what you want? Are those efforts effective?
23. On a scale of one to 10, how well do you feel you're using your mind's potential?

responds by purring or sighing or rolling over to let you scratch his belly. Indeed, that combination is so potent that some prisons have incorporated pet raising in their programs as one way of raising self-esteem, lessening conflict, and impacting criminal tendencies or mind-sets.

Of course, we can mix and match all this mood-enhancing sensory input. A candlelit steak dinner with Stan Getz's jazz samba playing in the background looks soothing and pretty, sounds lovely, and smells and tastes great. Hold your partner's hand during dinner, and you've got all the bases covered. But you can also break out of your norm and combine this sensory input in unexpected ways. Sample some lemon oil while listening to the Beatles, or savor your favorite steak sauce during Beethoven's Ninth. Lick ice cream while in the shower, or better yet, while standing in a storm in the middle of a beautiful park, field, or forest, listening to the raindrops fall. Remember how getting out of bed on the "wrong" side or reading a magazine you normally wouldn't pick up can help trigger new associations? Well, so can these new and unexpected sensory combinations.

When it comes down to it, you'll never know how using mind tools to tap your hidden mental powers can better your life unless you give it a whirl. How do you know you can't imagine what some-one else is drawing? Have you tried it? When your spouse is at the store and you're at home craving chocolate ice cream, have you tried sending the chocolate ice cream thought and seeing what happens? Or do you sit and home and think, "Eh, he won't get it"? The point is TRY IT. Otherwise you'll never know what you could potentially accomplish. Just don't forget to enjoy while you're at it. As I hope you discover, your brain is the part of your body that is the most fun to play with—really! So use the following mind games, not only to expand the capabilities of your mind—thereby making your world a richer place to be—but also to have fun in the process.

CARDS ANYONE?

Find a willing partner—or even a slightly skeptical and unwilling partner—to try the following exercise.

Use an ordinary deck of playing cards.

Take five cards and hold them out in front of you as though you were holding a poker hand. Do not show them to your partner. Look at the cards you are holding and choose one on which you will concentrate.

Have your partner place his index finger about 6 inches above the card fan. With the hand that's not holding the cards, grab hold of his wrist. Now, concentrate on one card and try to project it into your partner's mind for approximately 10 seconds. After 10 seconds, have your partner lower his index finger and select the card he thinks you're thinking of. Without even seeing the faces of the cards, he is trying to telepathically select the correct one.

Once he's selected one, you can let go of his wrist and tell him if that's the card you were thinking of. Repeat this game 10 times. Two correct answers is average, three to four is above average, five or more is exceptional. Switch roles.

Done? Did you get any right at all? If yes, then you have achieved communication without words.

HIDE-AND-SEEK

You can try this out on a group of friends tonight. You state that you would like to play a game of hide-and-seek on an intellectual scale, counting upon their mental efforts to guide you. As the "receiver" of their impressions, you will need the assistance of one person as a "sender" of their combined thoughts or impulses.

The choice of a "sender" is entirely up to them. That gives the game an immediate impetus. You are quite safe in this procedure, for unless most of the group is interested, they will not want to proceed at all. If skeptics surround you, the whole idea will die before it even starts because skeptics are interested only in voicing

---

MIND BUILDER

Board games like Scrabble, Othello, or Cranium that call not only for friendly competition but insight as well are a terrific way to stimulate your brain.

their own opinions, so if they are in the majority, they will simply dispute among themselves.

So, having roused the interest of a somewhat sympathetic audience, you will find that they invariably elect a cooperative person to work with you. If they don't, why bother? After all, it is just a game. You don't care if you lose, but you would, of course, like to win. With that attitude, intuitive games are the sort that you will never lose.

Generally, the group will give you a choice of partners, so be careful about that. You don't want someone who is so overwhelmed by the word intuition that they expect nothing short of miracles. A "sender" of the opposite sex is definitely attractive, but sometimes too much so. Your job is to keep your mind on mind reading. In this game of mental hide-and-seek, the "sender" is to be the "hider," while you, as the "receiver," will become the seeker. Ask your friends to hide an object: a ring, a paper clip, a hairpin, or whatever else they may choose. Tell them that you will leave the room while the article is being hidden. That job is delegated to the person who is the "hider," though the group themselves decide where the object will be concealed, such as beneath a wastebasket, under a sofa pillow, or behind a book on a shelf.

So you leave the room, and the object is chosen and hidden as described. Then you are called back, and you ask the "hider" or "sender" to stand at your right side. Grasp the sender's left wrist between your right thumb and fingers, as though taking a person's pulse. Maintain a gentle and even pressure, as you must be alert and as sensitive as possible to the slightest movement of the sender.

Your own mind must be receptive while you concentrate on finding the object. First, begin to move about the room, and as you do, follow the slightest pressure, even though you are not sure that you actually feel any but are only imagining it. You should cover most of the room, including the out-of-the-way corners, as this not only keeps the group tense and interested but enables you to compare those impressions.

If you lead the sender in a wrong direction, that is, *away* from the hidden object, you will feel an almost imperceptible tug *toward* the hiding place. Slowly but surely, these minute tugs will lead you to the object. Often, when you first play this game, you will be more amazed than the other players, particularly when you reach the hiding place and actually find the object. The person most mystified is usually the sender, who has no idea that he—or she—is guiding you, the receiver, along your way. For that reason, you should make sure that the sender is both serious and sensitive, capable of concentrating on the object and thus helping you mentally but without consciously providing any physical impulse.

You can have other people play this game of psychic hide-and-seek, both as senders and receivers, and you will find that most of them will agree that at times, there actually seemed to be a transfer of thought from one subconscious mind to the other, without any other form of noted communication.

JUST THINK!

This game is an extension of the game above. Explain that an object is to be hidden much as before, but that after the hider has placed it in the chosen spot, and *while you are still absent from the room,* the group decides upon some other place where you are to put the object after you have found it. This means that the sender must subconsciously provide you with *thoughts in sequence* in order to carry the game through to its conclusion.

This is an impressive and challenging demonstration. Suppose that the object is a paper clip hidden beneath an ashtray and that you find it in due course. The onlookers may feel that the sender has led you to it, but when you continue to rove the room and finally place the clip on a book that is lying on a table—exactly where everyone has been willing you to put it—the group gains the impression that you, the receiver, have led the sender to the final spot.

Actually, the sender is still guiding you. Whenever you are in doubt, do not wait for the sender to guide you. Instead, make moves of your own, so that the sender can resist them and draw you back to the right course. When you find the chosen object, if you are hesitant about picking it up, you will feel the sender drawing you to it.

Once you have picked it up, if you start to replace it when you should take it somewhere else, you will again experience that resistance—often mentally, rather than physically—indicating that the sender is trying to draw you along the way. So you go along, again changing direction at intervals, in order to encourage that same resistance that is so important.

Placement of the object is often quite a climax, denoting real accomplishment on your part. Actually, it is a fulfillment of a mental wish or purpose. But again, you can verify the impulse by drawing away—so slightly that your action is imperceptible—only to have the sender draw you back. Once you have put the object where it belongs, resistance ends, and you can say, "That's it."

There is another factor that begins to evidence itself once you add the more complex feature of thoughts in sequence. That factor is group intensity. You will find that many people join the game as mental participants, seriously *willing* you on to your goal as ardently as if they were playing the part of sender. At times, the whole atmosphere seems to be telepathically charged. This can be a help at crucial moments.

However, you must warn people against becoming unduly restless or whispering among themselves. An audible clue or a single spoken word can defeat the purpose of the game, which is to guide by thought impressions only, even though subtle physical aids are involved along with intuitive insight.

As already mentioned, you can expand participation in the psychic game by choosing new "senders" and letting players take turns as "receivers" so that they can individually enjoy this highly gripping experience.

FOUR-FINGER LEVITATION

You'll need five people and one chair for this game.

One person sits in the chair. One person stands to the left front side of her. One person stands to the right front side of her. One person stands to the left back side of her. One person stands to the right back side of her. Clasp your two hands together and extend your index fingers. The two people in front place their index fingers underneath her knees. The two in the back place their index fingers under her arms (armpit). Now test how heavy the person is by trying to lift her up. Chances are you can't do it.

Once you've verified that you can't lift her up, remove your hands. Have her close her eyes and slowly count to 10, telling her to imagine she is getting lighter, lighter, light as a feather, weighing nothing. Then the four of you close your eyes and count slowly to 10, picturing yourselves getting stronger and stronger, lifting her up effortlessly.

When you reach 10, open your eyes. All four of you put your fingers back where they were when you originally tried to lift her up. Then count to three out loud. At the count of three LIFT HER WAY UP INTO THE AIR. She will literally soar upward. She will feel incredibly light and you will be surprised at how easily you lift her. Try it!

DISAPPEARING ACT

Next time you go outdoors, find a cloud. Now concentrate on it and imagine it becoming a shape. This is part of your creative process at work, as well as your concentration ability. Now try to make it disappear. Say to yourself, "I want that cloud to diminish, to disintegrate, to dissipate, to finally disappear altogether." As you concentrate on the cloud, you will find that it actually disappears. Coincidence or the power of your mind? Try it. Then you tell me. Either way, the effort that you put into concentrating is an exercise of great importance.

REMOTE VIEWING? . . . OR MAYBE NOT

Back in the 1970s, some unusual ESP experiments were conducted at the Stanford Research Institute in California. One series of tests was called "remote viewing."

The test involved two subjects, a sender and a receiver. The receiver remained in the laboratory while the sender got into a car and drove to a randomly selected location. When he arrived at the location (either outside or inside), the sender observed the surroundings and tried to transmit it telepathically back to the receiver. The receiver at the laboratory then tried to describe what the sender was viewing.

The receiver wrote down or drew what he thought he was sensing. The sender then returned to the laboratory and the results were compared. This series of experiments resulted in some seeming hits.

Tests were also conducted for the military, in which a receiver in the United States tried to remotely view the former Soviet Union's nuclear missile installations and describe the installation sites. Again, the results were uncannily correct, lucky (or had other factors been at work).

You can try remote viewing experiments yourself. There are three ways to do it:

1. Get a friend and designate a time to project. At the appointed time, the receiver then attempts to tune in on what the sender is

FINAL MIND BUILDERS

Question: What is special about the number 854917632?

Answer: It contains the numbers one to nine, in alphabetical order.

Question: Two boys and a man need to cross a river. They can only use the canoe. It will hold only the man's OR the two boys' weight. How can they all get across safely?

Answer: The two boys go across. One of them gets out. The other one goes back. He gets out and the man gets in. He goes across. Then the man gets out and the other boy gets in and goes across. Then the boy who was left gets in and now they both go across together.

Question: A says to B, we were born the same year, month, day, and minute. We were born in the same hospital room and we have the same two parents. We are not twins and we have no brothers. Explain this.

Answer: They have a sister C and they are triplets!

WHAT PIECE OF FURNITURE IS DEPICTED ON PAGE 224 IN THE APPENDIX?

I KNEW YOU COULD DO IT!

experiencing. The receiver should make sure to write or draw all impressions while the sender writes down everything being observed. Then compare the results.

2. If you don't want to set up a time and go through the physical journey to conduct the experiment, sender and receiver can be in the same room. The sender simply takes a journey in his mind. In other words, he imagines he is in a certain place, viewing the surroundings and transmitting it to the receiver. Pick a place that's familiar to the sender. It may be a recently visited location or a place from the past. If you can't think of one, make one up. Some suggestions: a forest, mountain, stadium, museum,

school, library, building, foreign country, home, park, etc. Whichever way you go, the receiver writes down his impressions, and the results are compared. Then switch roles.

3. Use postcards. Go to your local stationery store and buy 10 to 20 picture postcards. Make sure they are all different and contain a variety of locations. Mix them up and select one postcard. Concentrate on the image and, in your mind, pretend you've actually been transported to that location. Then try to project what you see to the receiver.

No matter which experiment you try, the sender needs to use as many senses as possible. In addition to seeing the surroundings, try to feel the temperature as well as the texture of wherever you might be, hear the sounds, taste the air or the flavors of the local cuisine. The more senses you put into play, the more accurate you become.

APPENDIX

PENDULUM ORB DIAGRAMS

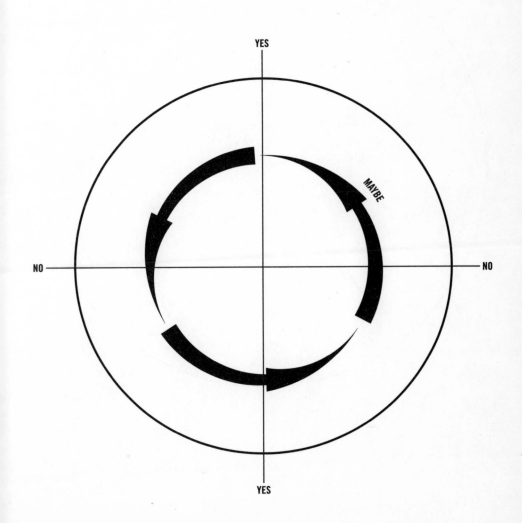

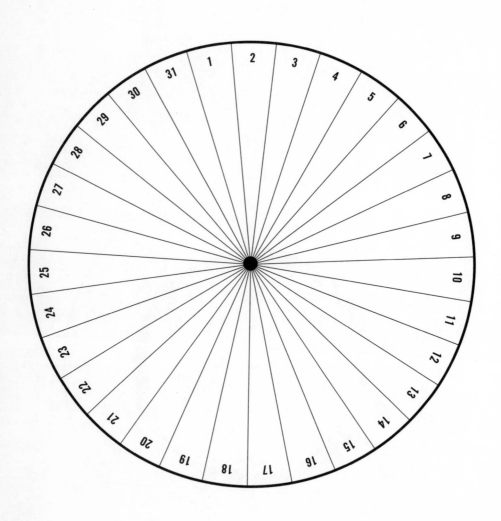

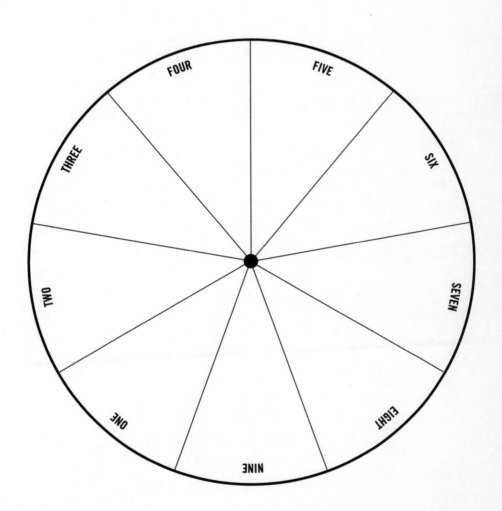

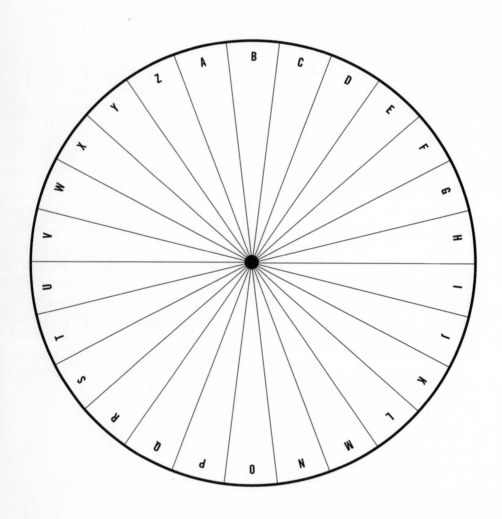

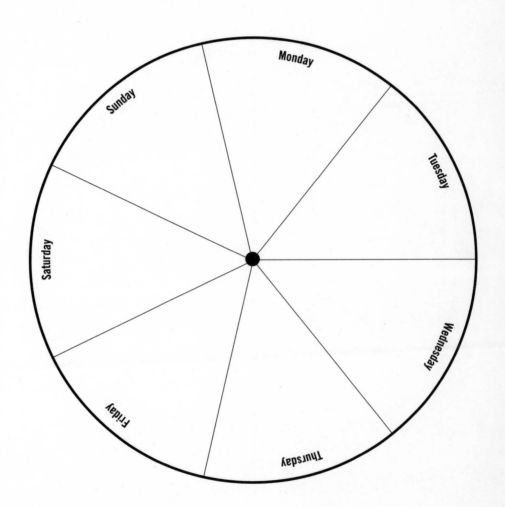

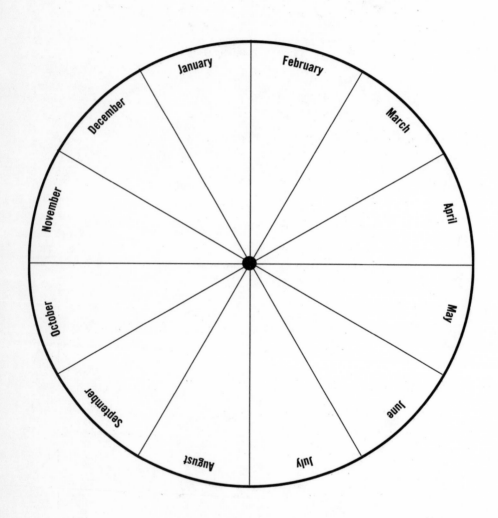

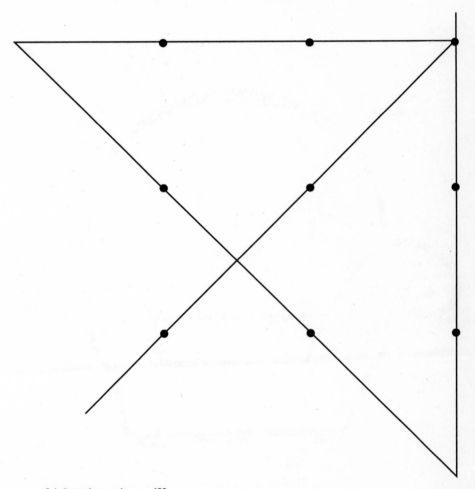

Solution to dot exercise on p. 160.

Car

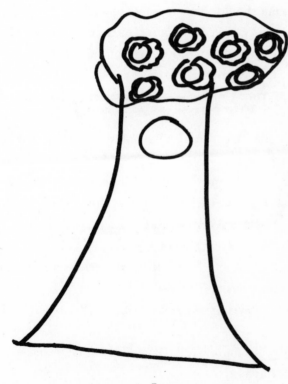

Tree

ACKNOWLEDGMENTS

I do not believe that there is any thought, idea, or philosophy that once experienced does not leave its mark. I am the accumulation of my life's experiences and interaction, most good, some not. So many have had impact on my thinking, and on me. Here are just a few that come to mind. I regret the absence of anyone who I did not mention but should. There are just so many.

From University of Pennsylvania: Ira Glasser, George Gerbner, Eric Swartz, Ray Birdwistell, Erving Goffman, Gregory Bateson, Bob Shayon, Gail Zivan

From New York University: Neil Postman, Susan Mausehart, Jay Rosen

The 13, particularly: Charles Reynolds, Marc Sky, Ted Karmolovich, and Gil Eagles

Performance colleagues and developmental influences: Lee Freed, Richard Mark, Richard Webster, Jon Fisher, Marc Paul, Craig Karges, Arthur Kurzweil, Bob Cassidy, Tom Deluca, Quentin Reynolds, Marc Wiener, Marc DeSousa, Max Maven, Maurice Fogel, John Pullum and other dedicated artists and masters of though too numerous to list.

Children's Television Workshop: Lewis Bernstein and Amy Wolfson

The Producers: Andrew Fell, David Richenthal, Anita Waxman, and Diane Terman

William Morris Family, especially: Betsy Berg and Mel Berger

Rodale: Zach Schisgal, Courtney Conroy, and Bill Phillips at *Men's Health* magazine

INDEX

Boldface page references indicate illustrations. Underscored references indicate boxed text, charts, and marginalia.